T0367319

Enabling the Disabled

How You Can Do a Better Job
Welcoming the Disabled to Your Church

REV. DR. THERESA C. TAYLOR

WESTBOW
PRESS®
A DIVISION OF THOMAS NELSON
& ZONDERVAN

Scriptures taken from the Holy Bible, New International Version®, NIV®. Copyright © 1973, 1978, 1984, 2011 by Biblica, Inc.™ Used by permission of Zondervan. All rights reserved worldwide. www.zondervan.com The "NIV" and "New International Version" are trademarks registered in the United States Patent and Trademark Office by Biblica, Inc.™

This book is a work of non-fiction. Unless otherwise noted, the author and the publisher make no explicit guarantees as to the accuracy of the information contained in this book and in some cases, names of people and places have been altered to protect their privacy.

WestBow Press books may be ordered through booksellers or by contacting:

WestBow Press
A Division of Thomas Nelson & Zondervan
1663 Liberty Drive
Bloomington, IN 47403
www.westbowpress.com
1 (866) 928-1240

Because of the dynamic nature of the Internet, any web addresses or links contained in this book may have changed since publication and may no longer be valid. The views expressed in this work are solely those of the author and do not necessarily reflect the views of the publisher, and the publisher hereby disclaims any responsibility for them.

Any people depicted in stock imagery provided by Getty Images are models, and such images are being used for illustrative purposes only. Certain stock imagery © Getty Images.

ISBN: 978-1-9736-4286-2 (sc)
ISBN: 978-1-9736-4285-5 (hc)
ISBN: 978-1-9736-4287-9 (e)

Library of Congress Control Number: 2018912260

Print information available on the last page.

WestBow Press rev. date: 10/23/2018

Blessed are you who never bid us "hurry up"...
often we need time rather than help.
Blessed are you who take time to listen... if
we persevere, we can be understood.
Blessed are you who ask for our help, for
our greatest need is to be needed.
Blessed are you who... don't expect me to
be saintly just because I am disabled.
Blessed are you who understand that
sometimes I am weak and not just lazy.
Blessed are you who forget my disability of
the body and see the shape of my soul.
Blessed are you who see me as a whole person...
not as a "half" and one of God's mistakes.
Blessed are you who love me just as I am without
wondering what I might have been like.

Taken, with deep appreciation, from the
poem "Beatitudes for Disabled People"
By Marjorie Chappell

This book is dedicated to my best friend and husband, Ken. You wear so many hats and yet you carry out each job with so much love, humor and zest! Whether you are picking up the pieces from my meltdowns, or proof reading for the 100th time. You make me feel complete. You make me feel that I can do anything with you by my side. Your love for Jesus is so infectious. You have an amazing gift of meeting people where they are at, no matter if that is a homeless person on the street, or a businessperson in a boardroom. You approach each situation with such authentic compassion and commitment that Jesus shines through. Thanks for taking this crazy adventure with me.

Contents

Acknowledgements xi
Preface...xv
Introduction...xvii

CHAPTER ONE...1
I Didn't Ask for This Job

CHAPTER TWO..8
This Book is Actually Good News

CHAPTER THREE 30
What It's Really Like

CHAPTER FOUR...49
Sawubona

CHAPTER FIVE 73
Some Strategies for Success

CHAPTER SIX 93
Teach Second-Class Citizens of the World the Privileges
and Responsibilities of Being First-Class Citizens of Heaven

CHAPTER SEVEN 119
A Little Help with the Americans With Disabilities Act

CHAPTER EIGHT 131
A Final Word about God's Grace

About the Author...141
A Little List of More Resources.. 143
Notes 145

Acknowledgements

Oak Hill Baptist church has played a vital role in forming my attitudes of acceptance in a local church. From the moment I first walked through their doors and still today, even though I live 1,100 miles away, they still provide an abundance of love, prayers and Christian fellowship. Every time I go back to visit it is like coming home again. Thanks for being so loving and for believing in me.

International Ministerial Fellowship has been an integral part of my professional and spiritual life as a pastor. They are faithful prayer warriors and provide excellent council on a wide range of topics. Most of all it is fantastic to know that someone has your back and if life seems impossible, they will continue to point me towards Jesus and ask how they can help.

Thanks to Bethel University and Seminary in St. Paul, Minnesota, for cultivating an environment of learning and growth. Regardless of my disability I have been academically challenged to keep thinking outside of the box. They have helped me to evaluate myself in numerous areas in order to show me how I can improve and better serve the Lord in ministry.

I am also very thankful to the Louisville Institute for providing excellent grant opportunities to help me make the dream of publishing this book come true. Their financial assistance allowed me to focus my attention on gathering information for the book. It is also wonderful to see the Institute's desire to support ministry leaders make kingdom changes that will also bring about social changes.

I am also so incredibly grateful to the Chaves family! Our friendship has been an incredible blessing. Their love for the Lord is genuine and it is wonderful to live communally with a family that keeps its eyes on Jesus. Their support and love through challenging times reminds me of how God intends heaven to be. I feel loved and affirmed for just being me. Thanks for being so willing to share your lives with me. Each of you is a treasure!

I want to thank my parents (Ben & Carol Beers) and my brother (Tim Beers), for never thinking that an activity was impossible for me to do. When I went from low vision to totally blind, you made it possible for me to stay in my regular school. You were always willing to adapt things to help me out. You never stopped me from trying something new. You always believed that I could do whatever I wanted to do. Thanks for giving me this foundation to keep reaching for my dreams!

Thanks to my 3 fabulous children (Nick, Chris, and Amanda) and two terrific granddaughters (Aliza & Aron)! I spent much time researching and preparing the materials for this book. When you all still lived at home you were supportive in sharing my time. You made sure I had writing snacks. You also created great diversions by playing games with me and by binge watching a show or two. Now that you are all on your own, I still appreciate your positive outlooks. I am so proud of what you have grown into. I know that each of you will also make your dreams come true and will make this place, here on earth, better for others to live. Keep looking past people's differences and continue to fight for social equality for all regardless of society's labels. I love you to the moon and back!

Words cannot adequately express how thankful I am for Andrew Gross, my editor. You have an amazing gift to sort through my ramblings and make them understandable. You know how to keep my voice and still polish things up. Through both my doctoral thesis and this book you have been amazing at helping me to see the end result of a project finished. More importantly, you've helped God be glorified through this book! There have been numerous struggles, but your patience, wisdom and love for the Lord has helped make this book a reality. Thanks for believing in this subject enough to stick through the hard times! Blessings to you and your family!

Preface

Are there persons with disabilities sitting in your pews on Sunday morning? Whether your answer is yes, no, or I really do not know, this book will provide you practical strategies for not only welcoming the disabled into your flock, but enabling the disabled to realize their esteemed place in God's kingdom. You will be given insight into why many disabled find church a stumbling block for growing closer to God.

My first experience with church as an adult was an incredibly awesome one. But knowing what I know today I am humbled to say that statistically my positive encounter is highly unusual. Unfortunately, I realized the truth of these statistics as I continued to participate in ministry. 90% of persons affected by disabilities either have left their church due to discrimination or they simply have not attempted to visit a church due to all the negative stories they have heard from other disabled people.

I bring up my wonderful initial experience with church for a few reasons. First, I know what a loving, supportive church family looks like. Sure there are minor issues. But when you stay focused on what brings you and others closer to Jesus then the issues work themselves out. So I know without a doubt that every person with a disability can have this fantastic experience with a local church.

Second, I have experienced the pain and heartbreak of

rejection by a church. This perspective allows me to write candidly with you and let you know not only how it feels to be an outcast from a church, but also what will help to resolve these excluding behaviors.

God has uniquely equipped me to write this book. I have been disabled my entire life. There are several disabled people in my family. I understand the ups and downs of the disabled life. I also understand the language, accommodations and attitudes that are prevalent in the disabled population. This background allows me to speak with credibility about specific topics relating to disabilities.

God has also called me to be an ordained pastor with International Ministerial Fellowship. This call has prepared me to understand the dynamics of church leadership. I have served in ministry positions that let me see firsthand the inner workings of a church and a para-church ministry. I know the reality of budget constraints, volunteer shortages, architectural barriers and so much more. I realize that all of these factors and many more make up baggage for you to deal with. This is baggage that you as a church leader bring to the table as you look at how to better serve the disabled. I get it.

Think of my words in this book as an offering of reconciliation. Let me extend the olive branch from the disabled side and say that I am confident that you will be blessed beyond your wildest imaginations by reading this book and putting these ideas into your prayer life, into your teaching and preaching, and into your management of the church. You will be amazed at the magnificent potential you will discover among the disabled population. You and your church membership will be transformed by loving on the disabled who God calls the least of us. You will give many disabled people the hope of a perfect body in heaven. You will also be able to give them a supportive community so they can face daily challenges of living with a disability here on earth.

Introduction

Thanks for taking the first step towards welcoming the disabled into your church. This book will help you lead better, whether you are a pastor of a congregation or a Sunday school teacher. Maybe you have not found a ministry post yet in a church. Maybe you are thinking about how to reach out to a new group of faces. Wherever you're coming from, this book is going to be useful.

Whatever the reason you picked up this book, thanks! Be prepared for the many blessings that are just waiting to be showered over you and your ministry. Sure, there will also be times of embarrassment, awkwardness, helplessness and of course we cannot forget frustration.

I am not here to reassure you that this endeavor will be a piece of cake. As you will learn, many people affected by disabilities have been badly hurt by the church. This leaves them a little hardened and a lot discouraged, mixed in with some bitterness. This book will give some background information about the history of the disabled and the church. It will also provide some insights into other ways that the disabled have experienced rejection.

This commitment you are about to embark on may be full of trials, but I know without a doubt that the blessings and incredible joy that you and others will encounter will be beyond your wildest expectations. Remember, through it all, God makes it emphatically clear: the disabled are a crucial part of any church family. When you start welcoming them as such the outcomes will be mind-blowing.

One last point of wisdom that I would like to impart to you before you start reading this book. Remember, as long as you respond the way Jesus would respond, it will all be good. If you don't have all the answers, simply admit your lack of knowledge. If you are uncomfortable, ask for prayer. If you are frustrated, take a moment and remember the abundance of grace that God hands out in your life.

Now it is time to get ready and reach out to the largest unreached people group! They need and deserve to know the love of Christ. Take the first step and watch God be glorified in amazing ways!

Chapter One
I Didn't Ask for This Job

I didn't set out to be an advocate for the disabled. I didn't want the label "disability ministry." Honestly. When I was very young, starting at maybe around age eleven or twelve, I dreamed about working as an FBI profiler with troubled youth. My grandfather told me that life is a series of dreams and that each of us needs to work toward our dreams. FBI profiler was my dream. I had a heart for troubled youth even at that early age. The FBI seemed so interesting and, well, right up my alley. However, after many degree hours in my adult life, I learned this may have been my dream, but not necessarily God's.

In spite of my dream, God kept clearly directing me toward a ministry position. He didn't do a very good job convincing me of this at first, because I kept resisting. One reason I resisted was that His calling was to work with disabilities. Disabilities? God, are you serious? So, I kept digging in my heels, and I held on to a part of my dream by insisting to God that He wanted me to work as a youth pastor. Didn't that seem like a good compromise, God? Wouldn't God be reasonable if I were reasonable?

But God kept at it, setting up situations and encounters with people that moved me closer and closer to ministry with the disabled.

I will never forget one of these situations on an early Monday morning some years ago. I was sitting in a packed classroom at Bethel Seminary in St Paul, Minnesota when my indecisiveness about disability ministry reached a tipping point. This class counted toward my "Children and Family" focused Masters of Divinity degree. It was called "Advocacy for the Special Needs Family." It was just one stepping-stone toward earning my degree. At that time I already worked as a youth pastor in a local church setting. But the degree would equip me to do ministry better, and it would give me the credentials I needed for future ministry jobs. God, aren't You satisfied yet?

Ten weeks of this course were online. But this one week was held in-person at the Seminary. There were 22 of us that day and we were all new to each other. So the professor told us to introduce ourselves and to share an experience with disabilities. She asked us to relate our feelings about ministering to the disabled. I was next to last to share. I opened a *Diet Coke With Lime* and got comfortable so I could listen to my fellow students.

Classmate after classmate spoke of how those with disabilities drained their church budgets. Many recounted tales of how distracting a person with a disability could be during a worship service. Others mentioned that it seemed necessary to create a separate area just for the disabled attendees so the rest of the congregation would not feel so uncomfortable. There were not too many positive experiences shared that morning. Lord, was it really You putting me in this position in which I now found myself? It just felt too overwhelming to change all these hearts.

Finally, it was my turn to introduce myself, so I just quickly told the group my name and my place of ministry. But then the professor cleared her throat and said, "Don't you have more to tell us, Theresa?" I agreed, and proceeded to gush about my wonderful hubby and 3 kids. In my mind, I was done. But then she prompted me again to share about my experience with disabilities. I took a long sip of soda. We had been sitting for over an hour already and I could tell that my classmates were getting restless.

I said that I felt quite comfortable with many disabilities. Some heads perked up and some eyebrows were politely raised at that statement. But then interest turned to embarrassment, which in turn collided with what everyone had expected to gain from class that morning. Because that's when I quietly told everyone that I was totally blind and pretty deaf. The room got so quiet. I cleared my throat and went on to talk about the disabilities of my kids. Still, there was not a sound in the room.

We then had a break and I raced out of the room to beat the bathroom lines. Despite my best efforts to avoid them, many people stopped me on the way and apologized for their comments. Some of them asked me if they could help in any way. When I finally made it into the bathroom, I paused long enough to realize that my classmates genuinely wanted to hear my answers. I prayed for something helpful to say to them.

After the break, I reassured people that I did not take their concerns personally. I told them that their negative feelings were common sentiments. But I also told them it was time to change these excluding behaviors and attitudes.

What seemed to help my classmates the most that morning was my next statement, that this was a learning process for me as well. I let them know that there were many disabilities that I didn't understand either. I said that even though I am among the disabled, I still needed to remember how unique every person is and that there is not one solution that works for everyone. Working with the disabled means understanding a dizzying array of different accommodations and modifications, and no one has mastered them all. I shared with them that morning a phrase I'd read in another book: "We may be in different boats," I said, because I am disabled and you are not, "but we're in the same lake." In other words, even with my own disability, I could relate to my classmates' mixed feelings about ministering with the disabled.

The 2010 World Census indicated that over 650 million people with disabilities account for close to ten percent of the world population.[1] This means that people with disabilities are the largest minority in the world. This number will continue to grow as the population ages.

To better understand these statistics, here is what the U.S. Census Bureau defines as a disability: "a long-lasting sensory, physical, mental, or emotional condition or conditions, that make it difficult for a person to do functional or participatory activities such as seeing, hearing, walking, climbing stairs, learning, remembering, concentrating, dressing, bathing, going outside the home, or working at a job."[2] Those are pretty wide parameters. Think of all the people you know who might fit into this definition.

Eighty percent of the disabled live in a developing country and the majority of these countries treat the disabled as their most disadvantaged members.[3] This means that disabled people have some of the worst access to resources and health care in countries that are already struggling to provide those things. It means that the disabled have the smallest and weakest public voice, making them the least able to change their situations for the better.

To give you a glimpse of how widely disability affects just Americans, think about this: thirty six million people with known disabilities reside in the United States. This equates to twelve percent of the U.S. population. This statistic does not include people who reside in an institution, are under the age of five or over the age of sixty-two.[4] Six and a half million U.S. citizens are blind. Americans with hearing disabilities account for two and a half million of the population. There are approximately nineteen million people in America with mobility issues.[5] Some of these people undoubtedly live near you, in some sort of group home, with their families, or semi-independently. In fact, the number of disabled individuals living in every neighborhood around the globe is growing. Clearly, disability has a broad impact.

Now look at this situation through the eyes of a Christian worldview. The 2013 Lausanne Committee for World Evangelism indicated that ninety percent of disabled individuals never attend a church service.[6] Another way to look at this is that only five to ten percent of the disabled have been reached with the Gospel, or are *effectively* evangelized.[7] Ninety percent of 650 million is 585 million unreached people. "If we were to place these ... people together, they would comprise the world's third largest nation."[8] That would be like having a nation larger than the United States with no Gospel presence or influence. Worse yet, according to the Lausanne Conference, this nation would have "the highest rates of homelessness, joblessness, divorce, abuse, and suicide."[9]

Anyone at any time may become disabled. This threat affects all people without discrimination. Disabilities are not limited to a particular ethnicity, gender or class of persons. What does all this mean about who makes up our church congregations? Where should our evangelism efforts go? Who ought we really be trying to impact with the Gospel?

Now personally, I had experienced almost no direct discrimination or exclusion in the church because of my disabilities. Up until graduate school, my encounter with the church had been a positive affirmation of my self-worth as an individual, regardless of my limitations. I concluded that church was always a positive place for people with disabilities. In my experience, so many people have welcomed and accommodated me. The church even let me do really cool stuff—my first ministry job was to organize the church library. This may not seem difficult to you, but as a totally blind person I did need some accommodations. Even so, on every level it was a successful first foray into ministry work, and I saw this as a sign of how churches were accepting toward the disabled.

But wow, was I ever naïve. After several years of professional ministry, I began to realize the error in my earlier conclusion. People began to tell me story after story about how they, as disabled people, were asked to leave worship services for being "too distracting." Others told me of how people in churches kept focusing on their disabilities instead of on them as people. In other words, churches couldn't get past identifying them as "that lady in the wheel chair" instead of identifying them as children of God. Instead of feeling included by the Christian community, person after person told me that church made them feel more isolated and alone than ever before. Some people I talked with felt outright bitterness at God and at the church for all the exclusion and rejection.

So, my husband Ken and I created Seek the Son Ministries. We wanted to bring the saving power of Jesus Christ to the disabled, to the very people who weren't being reached by churches because of discrimination. But we wanted to see more than just evangelism. We desired to "enable the disabled," as we like to say to each other. This means that we tried to discover ways for the disabled to become full participants in church life. We wanted churches to see the disabled as full-fledged "co-heirs with Christ" (Rom. 8:17, NIV. See also Gal. 3:29, Eph. 3:6),[10] as people with all the privileges and responsibilities of followers of

Jesus. Instead of the disabled merely being members of the Body of Christ in name only, we wanted to see them become members of His Body in practice. What's more, we wanted the disabled to see themselves this way too.

Ken and I felt especially prepared for this work. We were uniquely positioned to be a bridge between the church world and the disabled world. We understood that our own disabilities allowed us to identify with other disabled individuals. And we knew that my status as an ordained pastor equipped me to understand the needs of the church. Because I straddled both of these worlds, I felt I could see into the souls of both. I saw that both disabled people and the church needed to work toward acceptance of one another. Both could make improvements. I understood the importance of giving a voice to the disabled. I also understood the need to refrain from blame in this reconciliation process, much to the great relief of the churches with which I've worked. Through Seek the Son Ministries, I have tried to bring the church and the disabled together.

That morning in my seminary class, it felt to me as if God were saying: "Theresa, I've clearly shown you the need in My Church. What are you going to do about it?" Reluctantly, with a heavy sigh and another long sip of *Diet Coke With Lime*, I said: "I guess so, God. Let's do this thing."

Chapter Two

This Book is Actually Good News

Despite my reluctance to dive into disability ministry, and despite any reluctance you might feel about reading this book, I am happy to tell you that this book is actually good news.

This book is good news for you, and it's good news for your congregation. It is good news because disability ministry brings with it huge benefits—benefits that will improve your congregation's overall quality of life. Among these benefits is the fact that you will improve your ability to lead more like Jesus leads. It's good news because it will show you how to bring hope to more people than before. It's good news because it will show you how to activate an entire army of disabled believers into ministry. It's good news because, when we minister with the disabled, we experience a sense of closeness to the heart of Jesus that we can't get if we ignore "the least of these." God wants you and your congregation to experience these benefits. Instead of disability ministry setting you up for misery, I am pretty sure God wants you to read this book because He wants the best for you and your church.

I'M OVERWHELMED TOO

But before I can talk about these benefits, I need to assure you, just like I assured my Masters of Divinity class that Monday morning so many years ago, that I am right there in the trenches with you. I will be the first to admit that disability ministry can be very frustrating, even for me. It can be confusing, exhausting, anxiety producing, and even discouraging, for all kinds of reasons.

One reason it can be frustrating is the difficulty of keeping track of all the different kinds of accommodations and modifications needed for various disabilities. I have been doing disability ministry for several decades, and I can't keep it all straight. I'm supposed to be this expert, but I keep encountering new situations and disabilities for which I am unprepared. I've made lots of mistakes, through both ignorance and forgetfulness. For example, I have several quadriplegic friends who each need a different kind of assistance. But I can't always remember the details of what helps one person instead of the other. I get confused over how complicated their care can be, and I regularly mix up one person's needs with another's. And to be honest, the confusion tires me out.

It is embarrassing to admit, but all this makes me hesitate when I contemplate committing to a new friendship with a quadriplegic person. You see, I get so worried about protecting my investment and protecting my pride, that I can lose sight of what I will be missing if I avoid this interaction. If I avoid the interaction, I will miss the gift of their friendship. I will miss the insight of their understanding. I will miss the many ways of being blessed through their actions, which far outweigh my minor discomfort. So don't rob yourself of the joy of surrounding yourself with people affected by disabilities. Everyone involved will be showered with blessings in abundance. Be ready to have your socks blown off when you invest in a relationship like this.

Even so, disability ministry can start to feel uncomfortable or stressful if we try to accommodate all needs. Let's be honest—these relationships can be downright awkward as well as exhausting and confusing. And it is really normal for any person, even the most open-hearted and open-minded person among us, to avoid awkward situations and relationships. We all do it.

I can really relate because I like to avoid awkwardness myself. Just like you, whenever I face an unfamiliar disability I can feel myself pull back and hesitate with the relationship. So I understand it when others try, for example, to avoid sight words when talking with me. Instead of saying "Hey, did you *see* that show on TV?" a seeing person might say to me, "did you *catch* that show on TV?" This is of course a sincere and understandable attempt to avoid an awkward interaction.

So I can relate to a common feeling, a feeling you've probably had, that what is supposed to be just a regular conversation can feel like a minefield when it's with a disabled person. For instance, you might be speaking to someone who is in a wheelchair. You wonder how he's going to get over to the baptismal font for the baptism service. Is he going to walk part of the way with a cane? Is someone going to assist him? Or perhaps someone is deaf and you are curious how she enjoys the music in the service. As I'll explain in Chapter 5, questions to help educate yourself are just fine. Now, the person being asked may not feel like answering and that is fine as well. Either way, look past the disability and remember that this is another person. He or she is vulnerable and is looking for fellowship in your church. Embrace this opportunity to converse. And if you get a little embarrassed by the interaction, so be it. Nobody will be keeping a scorecard except you.

But I do understand the fear of awkwardness. I really get it, because I feel the same way so much of the time.

Even the simple act of holding open a door can be complicated if we think too much about it. Some people are physically unable to open a door and there may not be any adapted door buttons for easy opening. So in such a situation, do you offer to hold the door open or do you just do it and smile without being asked? It is not always an easy decision since you might feel that either the offer, or actually opening the door without being asked, could incite offense. You might worry that the other person will gripe: "Why do you think I need a door held open? Do you think something is wrong with me? Do you think I'm less than you?" Perhaps something like this has actually happened to you. So you'd understandably gun-shy to find yourself in the situation again. But then, does it feel right to simply ignore the person altogether?

I'll tell you a funny story about holding open the door. It involves one of my favorite topics: my kids. Chris is my middle son, and when he was around 11 he came to me and asked for advice on holding open the door for a girl. I was a little taken aback at his request for advice, but I asked if he had a specific example. He explained to me that his Sunday school teacher had told him that it is gentlemanly to hold open the door for ladies. He tried this with some girls but they got mad at him. Other people thought perhaps he was up to no good. Chris wanted to know what he was doing wrong. I realized from this that even the simple courtesy of holding the door open can be complicated, whether you are interacting with a disabled person or not. Hopefully this helps put it all in perspective again. I asked Chris, "was your heart in the right place?" He said he thought it was. So, I encouraged him just to do what feels right when he's in that situation again. The same applies to working with the disabled.

But all this is to assure you that I really understand the feeling of being trapped in situations in which there is no way to avoid awkwardness. I understand it because I've been in them so many times myself.

Like for many of you, this awkwardness and confusion produces anxiety in me. Let me tell you about a situation in which the anxiety can get really bad for me. When individuals struggle with a communication difficulty, like a speech impediment or difficulty vocalizing, I feel pushed out of my comfort zone. This is because, with my hearing loss and inability to pick up on visual cues, I worry about understanding what they are saying. If I'm talking with someone who has a communication disability, our methods of communication become even more limited.

Many people with vocalizing limitations need to use a communication board to carry on conversations. These boards can be very elaborate, or they can be as simple as letters on a sheet of paper. The person unable to vocalize will point to the first letter of the word and wait for your affirmation that you understand it. Well, one summer evening I was talking to a friend who needed to use such a device. Because of my own blindness, we needed a third person to let me know what letters were being pointed out. As you can imagine, this whole affair took a lot of time and energy.

Being the impatient person that I am, I tried to deal with my anxiety by guessing ahead of time what words my friend would choose. I began to burst out with my guess about his sentence before he could get to the end of his thought. In the moment I actually thought I was being helpful and efficient. But in response, my dear friend would start his whole sentence over, and we were back to the beginning. This became frustrating and confusing for me, since I didn't understand why he was wasting time by restarting the entire sentence from the beginning after I had helpfully concluded it for him. But despite my anxiety, I wisely chose not to express the frustration and confusion I was feeling. I decided to simply smile and ask what I was doing wrong. He then pointed to a message he had written out. My assistant read it and it said that this friend hated his thoughts being finished for him and that he would appreciate it if I would let him complete his own words in their entirety. Well, I apologized, gave him a quick hug, and we were back into our conversation. This time, I absolutely kept my guesses to myself.

Today, this friend and I still joke about my mistake that night, born out of my anxiety. My friend was using his own sense of humor to point out to me that I was taking away his voice. I was disempowering him. It may sound minor, but sometimes you just want the chance to speak for yourself. And in my anxiety that day I could have caused a big rift in the friendship. I should have caught on more quickly what was going on, because I know what it is like when people try to take away *my* voice. In my own experiences I am accustomed to people addressing my husband and not me. For example, waitresses in restaurants will often ask him what I want. Fortunately, my husband has a great sense of humor and he'll answer with some smart-alecky comment like: "I have no clue. She changes her mind more than me." Thank you Jesus for the grace of humor!

But instead of causing a disaster with my friend, God gave me the grace to choose an attitude of acceptance. Instead of continuing to shut down my friend with my impatient guessing, I simply chose to ask what I was doing wrong. And then I chose to accept his criticism and adjust my behaviors. This simple acceptance diffused my anxiety and made all the difference between us.

But disability ministry can be frustrating for more reasons than simple exhaustion, confusion and anxiety. I get really frustrated with the sad reality that, even among people with disabilities, there is so much excluding going on. For example, even though I am deaf-blind, the deaf culture at large does not welcome me due to the adaptations I use to communicate. My adaptations, like hearing aids and special voice-to-text recognition software, put me into a different category than those who use only sign language to communicate.

You see, the North American deaf culture does not look at itself as disabled, and therefore it does not see itself to be in need of adaptations. They use American Sign Language as their primary communication, and most have carved out a very self-sufficient life that way. Another way of looking at this is that ASL is an actual language for people who do not hear. Therefore, it is not an adaptation, but a form of communication. Braille, for example, is an adaptation for blind individuals to tactilely read a language. But ASL is its own full-fledged language.

This means that some deaf people, like me who use other methods, can be considered outsiders. In my case, I am very oral and so ASL does not work for me—I cannot see the signs made by others. Visual cues are essential for understanding ASL's meaning. The face plays a big role in inferring meaning for ASL practitioners, and obviously I cannot see faces.

So if someone is in my situation and is blind before he is deaf, most likely he will choose to stay oral and perhaps use some tactile signs. For the most part people like me rely on their first acquired skills. On the rare occasions in which I do use sign language, I use it in English order, which is different than how ASL is used by its practitioners. ASL is difficult to translate word for word and it doesn't normally go in the English order. It has its own set of rules and some single gestures can mean entire phrases or emotions. When someone like me does use English word order in sign language, he takes each word and makes it into a specific sign. It slows down ASL users and can irritate them. All this often excludes me from the deaf culture.

I must say up front that I am talking in sweeping generalizations when I mention this exclusion. Many individuals within the deaf culture can be very welcoming. But it is still deeply frustrating when it happens to me.

Even within the blind culture there are degrees of acceptance. I have been totally blind since I was ten years old. This has left me feeling very frustrated at events for the blind. This is because people are considered "legally blind" when their vision reaches 20/200, which is quite a bit of sight for some. But it means that even at an event for blind people, I am among the most blind. Practically, this usually means I need more help getting around than others. It means I need access to Braille translations, even if a majority of people at the event can get by without Braille. This can make me feel inferior, even with sincere attempts to include me. I end up feeling so incredibly left out.

It has taken me years to appreciate why this happens at blind events. I have learned to move past it, but I bring it up to let you know that it is crucial to continue dialoging about feelings of rejection. Ultimately, I know I am welcomed. But this sense of difference still pushes me into a negative mindset. Let's make sure people in our churches are reminded that they are welcomed. They still may battle these perceptions of rejection, but they do have the ability to look beyond it, especially when we communicate a sincere welcome.

The number of divisions within the ranks of the disabled can be overwhelming. For instance, there is a division among disabled people between those who can still drive and those who cannot. Those who do drive can often feel superior to those who can't. Or then there is the common stereotype about blind people held by many people who have limitations in their limb movements. They will often lump us blind people in with those who have cognitive disorders. This might sound irrational at first, but because totally blind people like me cannot read print, some consider us to have dysfunctional cognitive abilities. Is it an accurate label? Of course not. But was the intent malicious? Most likely not. Even so, as a blind person, it is a struggle to see past this negative labeling and into a person's heart.

SO, JUST WHAT ARE THESE BENEFITS?

You might be thinking at this point, "You're discouraging me Theresa. If I had already thought disability ministry was hard, your stories aren't exactly helping me get over my fears." That's fair. But I relate these stories because I want you to know that even after decades of working with the disabled of numerous descriptions, I will be the first to admit this isn't easy. I really do understand your frustration on this topic. You can see I've made plenty of mistakes, even with my sincere efforts. As I told my classmates all those years ago, I may be in a different boat than you because I'm blind, but you and I really are in the same lake. We're in this together. So give yourself some compassion and acknowledge that this is really hard stuff.

But despite the challenge, I believe the benefits outweigh the costs. So, just what are these benefits that I mentioned at the beginning of the chapter?

BETTER LEADERSHIP

First of all, disability ministry is good news because it will improve your own leadership. Now don't get me wrong—ministering with the disabled may or may not get you ready to be the CEO of a Fortune 500 company. But it will make your leadership a lot more like Jesus' leadership.

Think of how Jesus ministered to what He called "the least

of these" (Matt. 25:40, NIV). Did you know that about 75% of the recipients of Jesus' direct ministry were the disabled? Think through all the stories from the Gospels that you can recall just from memory and you'll see what I mean. Seventy-five percent. If that's the target of our Lord and Master, shouldn't it be ours too?

As a part of leading like Jesus, disabled ministry will help you grow in the all-important area of emotional intelligence. Daniel Goleman writes that having high "EQ," or emotional intelligence, is a greater predictor of leadership success than things like IQ and strong academic performance: "The abilities that set the stars apart from average at work cover the emotional intelligence spectrum: self-awareness, self-management, empathy and social effectiveness."[11]

In other words, it's emotional intelligence, not intellectual intelligence, which makes the difference between mediocre leadership and really good leadership. Among many other things, Jesus was far and away the most emotionally intelligent person ever to walk the earth. When we grow in EQ, we get just a little closer to imitating His approach to leadership.

Working with the disabled is one of the greatest opportunities in this life to improve your emotional intelligence, and therefore your leadership. It does this in several ways. First, it pushes you to develop your self-awareness and your ability to manage yourself. Self-awareness and self-management are the foundations of emotional intelligence. For example, when you find yourself frustrated with the slow pace of a person who has limited limb movement, this becomes a great opportunity to look inside yourself and ask, "*why* is this frustrating me so much? Do I *need* to respond with frustration to make this situation better?"

Or, let's say a person with disabilities is really trying your patience. Maybe this is a person who makes overly loud vocalizations at just the wrong times in the worship service. Since you know it would be inappropriate to lose your cool directly at that person, it forces you instead to look within yourself and ask: "*Why* is this bothering me so much? What am I really trying to accomplish when leading this worship service anyways? What's so important about it that I can't allow for these interruptions?" In this way, you practice self-awareness, which in turn makes you exercise self-management. This is how you get better at self-awareness and self-management. And the more self-aware you are, the more you can practice things like patience, calmness, gentleness, and wise word choices.

Working with the disabled also improves your leadership because it pushes you to improve your ability to express genuine empathy and social effectiveness, two of the other key elements of EQ. As you know, in order to show empathy, you need to discover what it is like to be in another's shoes. A lot of able-bodied people find this hard to do this with people who have disabilities, because it is hard to imagine facing the struggles that they face. But working with the disabled forces you to search inside yourself more deeply and to stretch your imagination more thoroughly in order to find connecting points. It gets you thinking and praying harder for insight into another's situation. In the long run, this work strengthens your ability to demonstrate empathy.

And remember, empathy is not the same thing as pity. Leaders who are motivated by pity for those they lead don't make good leaders, because pity can be deadly to everyone involved. I want to stress this point strongly: avoid pity at all costs in your leadership. When you pity someone, it implies that you have more power than she has. It implies that you're the superior one. This mindset leads to a paternalistic approach of helping others. This degrades rather than empowers the person who is suffering. Disabled people don't need any more degrading. They need dignity.

Right now I am ministering to someone who has terminal cancer. I know I need to keep my pity in check, because it won't help this person at all. Those who suffer need understanding, support and spiritual encouragement. My ministry toward them should not be motivated by pity, but by the overwhelming desire to convey God's love even in trying situations.

When my kids were younger, I gave them a set of questions to ask themselves so that they wouldn't end up pitying others. I told them to take a step back and ask themselves: "what if I absolutely despised this person? Would I still feel this need to protect them? Would I still feel this need to prevent them from fully experiencing the suffering in a given situation? Or would I step up to the task God is asking of me and put all feelings aside in order to minister the Gospel of Jesus?" If we can learn empathy instead of pity, we will dramatically improve our leadership.

If, as Daniel Goleman insists, these elements of emotional intelligence lead to more successful leadership, why would you not want to be more emotionally intelligent? Why would you not want your emotional life to more closely resemble Jesus' emotional life? And if you want to be more emotionally intelligent, why would you not want to do the kind of ministry that helps you improve it? Why would you avoid such an opportunity?

MORE HOPE, BIGGER IMPACT, MORE MINISTERS

Disability ministry is good news because you will bring more hope to more people than you ever have before. I don't know about you, but I entered ministry because I wanted to bring hope into peoples' lives. I think that's why a lot of people enter ministry. We get to do that with disability ministry. We can give hope to people who have been ignored, marginalized, voiceless, and outright persecuted.

Even though this is the original motivation for a lot of new ministers, all the heaviness of ministry can tend to choke out the sense that we're in the business of bringing people hope. Ministry's many challenges, setbacks and disappointments, which often feel more numerous than its successes, not to mention all the boring parts of our job, can stifle that sense that we're here to make a positive impact in peoples' lives for God's Kingdom. This stifling effect creeps in slowly, so most of us don't even notice it happening. But gradually, many ministers adjust their expectations lower about their impact until eventually they find they are bringing hope to fewer and fewer people. However, when you minister with the disabled, there is an immediate certainty that you are making a difference in the lives of others.

One way you bring hope to the disabled is that you give them a voice. Because the disabled are treated as second class citizens in most places around the world, including here in the United States, most feel as though they have no voice. But when you confer on the disabled the dignity of being a child of God, the dignity of *first class* citizenship in heaven, of having all the privileges and responsibilities entailed in that citizenship, you automatically meet a felt need for a voice.

By restoring this dignity to people who are, at best, treated as second-class citizens everywhere else in society, you will unleash an entire army of believers into active ministry. Most pastors would kill to get their congregations out of the pew-sitting, consumer mentality. Most would kill to get their congregation members to see themselves as ministers with real contributions to make. When disabled people finally find their voice and become empowered to contribute to Christ's people, you'll find they become some of the most consistent, hardworking, dedicated and skillful lay ministers that a church pastor could ever wish for. Believe me, this is an army you want to unleash.

REV. DR. THERESA C. TAYLOR

A MORE LOVING CONGREGATION

Disability ministry is good news because it can help make a congregation more loving. More than any Bible study I've ever done or led, more than any inspiring sermon I've ever heard or given, more than any special ministry initiative I've ever witnessed or launched, working with the disabled moves people to be more loving. It can move the people in your congregation to be more loving too, if you'll let it.

It begins when you let the disabled share the stories of their lives. Nancy Eiseland argues that the everyday stories of the disabled, of those who have, as she puts it, "unconventional bodies," will help break down barriers of prejudice between people.[12] She contends their stories can be the starting point for reconciliation between people. Don't you want your church to be a place where barriers between people are removed? Where people learn to love one another despite their physical differences? Where people in the church can find real life examples and inspiration for reconciliation?

Yes, I know the objection that comes next. If you let the disabled share their stories, won't that just uncork a lot of complaining and whining? Won't disabled people just use it as an excuse to gripe and rant about all their problems? A lot of church members worry that this kind of sharing will fray a church's social fabric. Many worry that it will worsen a situation in which disability ministry already is larger, more expensive, and more time- and energy-consuming than a regular church can afford. They are afraid it will be so depleting that people won't have the wherewithal to love one another. So, how exactly will disability ministry help people to become more loving?

Believe it or not, an environment in which disabled people can share about their struggles provides one of the best possible opportunities for a congregation to grow in love.

I'll explain by pointing out how the Apostle Paul shared his own disability with the Corinthians. Yes, Paul had a disability. He described it in 2 Corinthians 12:7-10, calling it his "thorn" in his flesh. We don't know exactly what the disability was. Scholars have conjectured all kinds of things about it. Some think it could have been epilepsy. Others say it was migraines. Still others insist it was an eye condition. Whatever its nature, many agree it is a blessing that we do not know the exact illness. Not knowing allows all who struggle with a difficulty to feel included in Paul's story and to learn from it.[13]

Why did Paul reveal his disability to the Corinthians? You see, they did a horrible job loving one another. Many of Paul's teachings and rebukes to the Corinthians had to do with their failure to love each other. Look further at 1 Corinthians 1:10-13, 6:1-8, and 11:17-34 for yourself. Carefully examine the whole flow of Paul's argument throughout chapters 12-14. To counteract their terrible track record of loving people, Paul wanted them to observe several things.

First of all, Paul's struggle was a personal example of how difficulty can transform someone into a more loving person. Rather than growing bitter with his lot, Paul credited the disability with transforming his own heart. You see, Paul eventually learned to be grateful for his disability. He explained that it kept him from becoming "conceited" (2 Cor. 12:7, NIV), and it allowed him to experience the all-sufficiency of God's grace more deeply (12:9). He discovered that when he was weak and had come to the end of himself, he was mysteriously made strong in Christ and more able to experience God's power (vv. 9-10). This is the kind of transformed heart that is able to love others. What's more, Paul expected Christians to imitate his example of embracing weakness (1 Cor. 4:16).

Beyond personal transformation, Paul's vulnerability validated those Corinthians who struggled with weaknesses of their own. Look at 1 Cor. 11:17-34, when Paul rebukes them for their divisions and their bad handling of the Lord's Supper. He says that they humiliated "those who have nothing" (vs. 22, NIV) when the wealthy Corinthians ate before the poor Corinthians. In contrast to the Corinthians, here is Paul, the mighty Apostle, in his second letter exposing his own weakness, showing his solidarity with those who have nothing. This confirms the important place of those who are weak and who apparently have less to offer.

Paul's admission of his struggle also shows that it is acceptable in church to cry out because of one's pain. So many churches don't want to deal with the disabled because they find it unseemly for their needs to be put on display. It seems out of place in an environment like church that is supposed to be dignified. But by crying out because of his distress, Paul shows the church that the disabled can and even should make their needs known. Paul wasn't just going off on a bitter rant about his lot in life. He showed that it is appropriate for those in pain to share it with the church.

Most importantly, this example established that a relationship of mutual interdependence among believers is right and good. When the disabled share their needs and prayer requests, as Paul did with the Corinthians, it is a powerful way to encourage congregants to care for one another. The sharing gets a church's members to look out for one another and to sacrifice for one another.

Many people with disabilities hesitate to share their physical pains with churches because they are often met with exasperated comments such as "now what?" or "again?" I speak to disabled people all the time who tell me things like, "I feel like I'm a burden to the church." In response to these fears and anxieties, in this passage Paul models how he not only cried out to the Lord, but how he relied on his fellow brothers and sisters in Christ to assist him. The lesson from 2 Corinthians 12:7-10 is that it is acceptable for the disabled to struggle with and even complain to the Lord of their limitations. It is this struggle and complaint that results in personal transformation and deeper interdependence on other people. These traits in turn lead to a more loving congregation.

MORE ABILITY TO LIVE OUT PAUL'S "BODY" IDEA

Disability ministry is good news because it will help a congregation understand what it means to live out Paul's "Body of Christ" idea. I'm sure you're familiar with Paul's body metaphor in his first letter to the Corinthians. I'd wager a bet that you've preached on it at least once or twice. In Chapters 12 and 14, Paul describes how the diversity of gifts and strengths unexpectedly create a unity. This unity is unlike anything that the world can create. The best the world can come up with is uniformity, where everybody is the same. That's a pretty poor substitute for God's idea of unity in diversity. Through disability ministry, your church can get closer to the real thing.

When you make sincere efforts to do disability ministry, you are on the road to living out Paul's body metaphor. Isn't that a worthy goal? What if you could help your congregation move closer to living this biblical standard of the "Body of Christ"?

I want to zero in especially on Paul's discussion of weakness in 1 Cor. 12:21-26. This passage speaks of weakness in general and not disability in particular. But its point is still applicable to the disabled, since many disabled are among those who "seem to be weaker" (vs. 22, NIV) and who many "think are less honorable … and … unpresentable" (vs. 23, NIV). Here Paul emphasizes that every part (person) of a body is valuable and makes a necessary contribution, even though some church members may appear to be weaker than others. His point is that all types of abilities and gifts come together to make the Body of Christ, and you can't have the whole body if parts are missing.

Paul's idea is really astounding because, as he writes in verse 22, "those parts of the body that seem to be weaker are *indispensable*" (NIV). Indispensable? When was the last time you thought of disabled people as *indispensable* to your congregation? That means that your church can't do without them. Have you ever stopped yourself on a Sunday morning and said: "Hey, none of our disabled members are here today. I guess we can't really have church today, because they are *indispensable*"?

This is a critical starting point to dialogue about disability ministry. If those who appear weaker are truly indispensable as Paul asserts, then we need to move past the idea that our churches will be harmed by the extra work it takes to welcome the disabled. If the disabled are seen as a distraction instead of as *indispensable*, then we are really far away from living out Paul's metaphor.

MORE GRACE TO PERSEVERE IN SUFFERING

Disability ministry is good news because it will show your church how to experience grace and how to persevere in the midst of suffering. Now, not all disabilities may immediately bring suffering to your mind, since a disability can range from a minor inconvenience to a life-altering condition. But the reality is, whatever the degree of the disability, many of the disabled do indeed suffer. And many disabled people have discovered God's grace for perseverance in a way that many other people cannot even imagine.

In Paul's letter to the Romans, he talks about persevering through suffering in Chapter 5, verses 1-4. He outlandishly claims that the eventual outcome of suffering is hope. Many disabled people have discovered this to be true. So suffering can become common ground for the church and the disabled to begin to dialogue with one another. This is because even people without disabilities experience suffering. In fact, anyone who believes in Jesus will experience suffering and will be required to persevere. This means that everybody can relate to the suffering of a disabled person even if they have suffered due to different circumstances. Both parties can relate to the experience described in Romans 5 in which suffering strengthens faith and leads to hope. Consequently, both parties can relate to another.

Because this concept of suffering can be understood across all people groups, the topic will help to create a language to talk to people about specific hurts such as a disability, job loss, or death in the family. God teaches that faith in Jesus Christ brings about suffering and this leads to hope. This is life-changing encouragement for the disabled. Many times the church focuses on the disability. Instead, this focus can be on the hope in salvation.

The lesson I earlier drew from Paul's disability in 2 Corinthians 12:7-10 applies again here. As many commentators have pointed out, Paul's weakness was actually a power, a power that is nothing less than the Spirit working through believers.[14] Paul found his own physical weakness so important for ministry that he actually rejoiced to accept its challenges and its opportunity for perseverance. For Paul, the reward of persevering far outweighed its cost. He wrote earlier in the letter:

> *Therefore, we do not lose heart. Though outwardly we are wasting away, yet inwardly we are being renewed day by day. For our light and momentary troubles are achieving for us an eternal weight of glory that far outweighs them all. So we fix our eyes not on what is seen, but on what is unseen, since what is seen is temporary, but what is unseen is eternal.*
>
> 2 Corinthians 4:16-18, NIV

REV. DR. THERESA C. TAYLOR

Both disabled and non-disabled believers today can take heart that God is revealing His power through their suffering and weakness. Their weakness is actually an avenue by which God demonstrates His power, just as other kinds of suffering do in the lives of the non-disabled. As Paul shows us, disabled believers can rejoice in this challenge. This commonality of suffering, and how it points a path toward eventual hope and joy, is really good news for your church.

JESUS' HEART

Ministry with the disabled is good news because we experience a closeness with the heart of Jesus that we can't get any other way.

Now, I do not mean to say that disability ministry is your ticket to *feeling* close to Jesus. If that's your motivation, you're going to be sorely disappointed. If you haven't discovered yet that doing ministry to get good feelings is a recipe for burnout, then you've got a rude awakening ahead. You certainly won't last very long with that sort of motive.

What I am saying is that your heart will be more in line with the heart of God. Whether you can feel it or not is really irrelevant. But you can console yourself that this kind of ministry is right in the center of God's concerns.

I've already mentioned how Jesus made the disabled a focal point of His earthly ministry. As I've said, a good 75% of the people to whom He ministered were disabled in one way or another. And Jesus burned with jealous rage over their protection and care. For instance, do you remember how angry Jesus got in Luke 13:10-17 in defense of a disabled person? In that story, Luke writes that the synagogue leader was indignant that Jesus healed a woman on the Sabbath who had been bent over for 18 years. Jesus was livid at the synagogue leader:

You hypocrites! Doesn't each of you on the Sabbath untie your ox or donkey from the stall and lead it out to give it water? Then should not this woman, a daughter of Abraham, whom Satan has kept bound for eighteen long years, be set free on the Sabbath day from what bound her? NIV

Or what about when Jesus got angry and "deeply distressed" because several onlookers disapproved of His healing a man with a withered hand on the Sabbath (Mark 3:1-6, NIV)? To this day, Jesus' heart wells up in righteous indignation at the hypocrisies of those who refuse to lend a hand to the disabled while enjoying all the comforts of faith for themselves.

The love that Jesus Christ showed the disabled serves as a model for us today. It shows us how to love others no matter what. Modern day laws, regulations, protests, and bitter feelings will not display this love. But ministering to the disabled will. I am living proof that when the church follows Jesus' command to include and love the disabled, then others can "taste and see that the Lord is good" (Ps. 34:8, NIV).

Think about the story Jesus told of the Great Banquet in Luke 14:12-24. In this passage Jesus teaches the importance of welcoming all to the Great Banquet. In the story, the Master said to his servants: "Go out quickly into the streets and alleys of the town and bring in the poor, the crippled, the blind and the lame" (vs. 21, NIV). God has a special place in His heart for the "poor, the crippled, the blind and the lame." This story messes with our priorities, doesn't it? Even in the church we are inclined to invite only our "friends," our "brothers or sisters," our "relatives," or our "rich neighbors." We do this so that we'll get "repaid" here and now (vs. 12). But Jesus promises that we'll be repaid at the resurrection (vs. 14), not now.

We also hesitate to welcome the disabled because we imagine that if we do, we won't be able to handle all the new problems. But in the parable, the servant says, "there is still room" (vs. 22, NIV). Welcoming the disabled doesn't overextend God, who always has more room for them.

And don't forget how Christians have always celebrated the brokenness of Christ as a sacrament. When we observe the Lord's Supper, we remember the Last Supper and we remember Jesus' death on the cross. We do this to recall the ultimate brokenness of God's one and only Son. Nancy Eiseland says that in the Lord's Supper we are celebrating a "disabled God."[15] But if we celebrate a disabled God, then why don't we celebrate disabled people? It is ironic that churches focus on the brokenness of Jesus Christ in the Lord's Supper, but more often than not fail to accept broken, disabled people in their midst. But if the individual life of a disabled person is a creation of God, and if that person's life reminds us of God's own brokenness, then it follows that we ought to embrace the disabled among us.

SUMMARY

God wants you and your congregation to experience all the benefits I've mentioned. Instead of disability ministry setting you up for misery, I am pretty sure God wants you to read this book because He wants the best for you and your church. It is going to improve your congregation's overall quality of life in God. But more than how this is going to benefit you and your church, this message is good news for you because you will know that you and your congregation will walk and live more in step with Jesus, more "as Jesus did" (1 John 2:6, NIV).

Chapter Three

What It's Really Like

To understand how your church can better welcome the disabled, you need to get a feel for what it's really like to be disabled at a typical church. So, I'm going to tell you some true stories of how some disabled people have experienced the church. I've picked stories that are real but also are representative of very common interactions between churches and disabled people.

Now, I'll be the first to admit that every single church is different, and there are some wonderful churches out there. I've been a part of some great churches myself—churches that welcomed me for who I am; churches that enabled me to know God personally; churches that showed me how to walk with God and how to live in community as a follower of Jesus. In fact, my whole concern for reaching the disabled started way back when I began to attend Oak Hill Baptist in the Twin Cities area of Minnesota. That's where I first fell in love with Jesus Christ. This relationship provided me with hope and with a sense of perspective that one day all my hurts would be eliminated in heaven. I've longed to share this good news with everyone ever since. I've especially longed to share it with those who have disabilities, since I know it would drastically change their lives for the better.

So, it was a good church that God used to spark this love affair with Jesus and with His good news. You could say that the church motivated me into this kind of ministry. It was a church that gave me this longing to dismantle everything that might prove to be a barrier between the disabled and this good news. Ever since I came to know Him, the idea of church has been a good idea.

But some churches erect barriers to the disabled instead of demolish them. I know it sounds crazy, since more than anyone else disabled people need barriers removed. But the fact remains that some churches, most of them unconsciously I'm sure, make it harder instead of easier for disabled people to get involved and connected. The result of this is that many disabled people associate church with pain. I acknowledge that most churches are probably clueless that they are afflicting any pain at all. But in spite of the cluelessness pain is what so many of us disabled people feel from churches.

It took me a while to figure all this out. My experience with church had been so transformative and positive that it was hard to imagine that it might not be that way for everyone. I worked in several ministries before I learned how often people with disabilities experienced church involvement as discriminatory.

The simple fact is that many churches exclude the disabled. Seek the Son Ministries receives emails and inquiries daily with questions about how to combat discrimination in churches. This discrimination spans all denominations. No one particular denomination or church tradition has been especially worse than any other.

Discrimination by churches may take many forms. For instance, it might include inaccessible buildings or a refusal to allow a disabled person to remain in a worship service. Roger,[16] father of a three-year-old boy with autism, was asked to leave the worship service. His son makes noises during the music. The elders felt it was degrading to the service. Roger's son was also excluded from Sunday school. Parents expressed concern that his son might teach their children these same vocalizations.

I wasn't surprised when I learned Roger's story, because I've heard from pastors and lay-leaders on several occasions that disabled people bring too much chaos and burden to churches. Therefore, they conclude, it is best if they simply do not attend the regular worship service.

Some disabled people are forbidden to engage in a particular ministry. Lisa talks of exclusion from the church choir. Her choir director feels Lisa's blindness could potentially cause harm to other choir members because getting to the choir loft requires traversing several flights of stairs. Lisa competently takes stairs in many other aspects of her life, but the director still insists she cannot participate.

Sometimes, people with physical abnormalities are avoided. Sometimes they are outright treated as second-class citizens. Tracy talks of her discouragement during greeting time. No matter how much she tries, people still refuse to touch her. She is unclear whether it has to do with her wheelchair or her disfigured hands. I've talked with others who have been asked to sit toward the back of the sanctuary so their disfigurement won't disturb other worshipers.

I've encountered conflicts in local churches over whether or not to serve the disabled at all. Often, one segment of a church's constituency will simply refuse to reach out to the disabled. It causes too many problems and is too great a burden they reason. Many conclude it is best not to serve them because their needs are just too great.

Sometimes these conflicts spread to whole denominations. They produce contradictory policies and approaches that confuse the disabled: are we or aren't we welcomed? In 1980 for example, the American Lutheran Church (ALC) attempted to create a theology of access for those with disabilities. It was a great idea, but instead they produced even more discrimination. Their general assembly put forward a resolution for inclusion of handicapped individuals.[17] This resolution was initiated by the United Nation's declaration to celebrate 1981 as the year of the disabled in the hope of helping improve their lives. The ALC created specific policies and curriculum to foster an atmosphere of compassion and acceptance for the disabled.

All this would make it appear as though the ALC was on the right track. But only a few years later, in 1986, this same denomination passed a resolution, "Seminary Admission and Certification Criteria in Relation to the Work ALC Pastors are Expected to Do."[18] This resolution barred several types of disabilities from ordination and admission to seminary. More specifically, it tried to restrict potential candidates based on their physical mobility and energy capacity. These conditions included progressive, degenerative neurological and physical disorders (e.g., multiple sclerosis, ALS, juvenile onset diabetes, cystic fibrosis, some kidney diseases, non-correctable heart conditions, quadriplegia, and severe psychiatric disorders).[19] These wide ranging classifications would exclude me from serving in the ALC.

The ironic tragedy of this incident is that a denomination worked so diligently to welcome and show love for the disabled but then denied the right of the disabled to fulfill the call to be pastors. I'm not sharing this story to shame the ALC, a denomination that merged with the Lutheran Church in America to become the Evangelical Lutheran Church in America in 1988.

I share it to point out how confusing church can be for people with disabilities. I ask the question once again: are we or aren't we included?

My own path to ordained ministry was filled with these same kinds of mixed messages. God clearly showed me over and over that He wanted me to become a pastor. After prayer and discussion with my senior pastor, I became licensed and met with several mentors to guide my steps as a pastor. I was excited about what God had in the store for my future and how I was being prepared to impact people for His kingdom. But during this process, something happened that left me bewildered.

You see, I was also working for a disability ministry at that time. It mainly involved teaching others how to welcome the disabled. I loved this work and I eagerly anticipated ways that I could serve. My hubby Ken and I love youth and so we decided to work at this ministry's camp that hosts families with disabilities. We filled out our applications and we waited excitedly to make memories with families affected by disabilities.

Unfortunately, this application process led to a lot of trouble. It ended up sparking a great deal of tension between the ministry and me, and it gave me a clear picture of how my disability is thought of more as a liability than an asset.

Months passed since we'd applied and I wondered why we had not heard yet about our camp assignment. It was well past the date when we were supposed to have learned about it. So, I made some phone calls and was met with hesitation and excuses. Then it started to sink in that my husband was welcome but I was not. I finally pressed a supervisor and he told me that it was against policy to allow a person with my type of disabilities to serve. They had these preconceived ideas that a person with no vision had no place assisting campers. I was saddened that nobody wanted to tell me the truth. Then after further pushing,

I discovered this was an unwritten policy. It was bad enough that they had this policy. The fact that they did not want to share it with me or defend why they had created it made it worse. But the worst part of it for me was that it was unwritten. This made it so that I didn't even have a way to challenge it.

I was hurt on so many levels. First, I was shocked to realize that I hadn't been informed about the rules governing our interactions with this ministry. We all know that when you enter a relationship, you need to know the expectations. But here I was, committing myself to a relationship with this disability ministry, and I couldn't even learn the expectations. Yet they avoided a healthy dialogue about their concerns. This meant that there wasn't even an opportunity to talk about how we might be able to work with them.

More than that, I was heart sick to know that the people with whom I was serving still held some antiquated notions of my abilities or lack of abilities. I was shocked, hurt and saddened that these people were the hands and feet and hearts of ministers serving the disabled. They are the future of welcoming the disabled?

I wanted to make the situation work. I valued these people and I wanted to make lemonade from all of these lemons. Unfortunately, it became the elephant in the room. We never were able to talk it out or process it. I decided not to walk away as of yet. I felt God was telling me to be strong and show grace and acceptance.

During this same time I became an interim youth pastor for my home church. I loved this position and felt blessed. God encouraged me to continue toward ordination. I did so. After my ordination council I planned a huge celebration for my vows. I wanted to include all who wanted to be there. I had chosen to be a minister with a nondenominational group. I was convinced that this would allow me to minister in several churches as the Lord showed me. Initially, my home church experienced sadness that I was not following that denomination, but we came to a mutual understanding.

As part of the celebration I wanted to include representatives from the disability organization with which I had served—the same organization that had denied my application at the camp. Since I had decided to follow Jesus in forgiveness, patience and acceptance, I was willing to put our past differences behind us. But when I sent them the invitation, I was shocked at the reply. I was told that they would not support my ordination. They felt that a woman should not serve as a pastor. They outlined specific criteria that they believed excluded me from the role as a pastor. Their criteria were so restrictive that they wouldn't even allow me to teach Sunday school.

So, here I was at this happy time of my life, and I was faced with a trial of betrayal. I had already worked for over two years for this organization and I had never hid the fact that I was a pastor and working toward ordination. Yet here I was, being told that they were against my ordination.

After tears of anger and sadness, I decided to leave the organization. My social justice side wanted me to scream and rant and get everyone angry at this group. Yet God quietly showed me His love and more importantly His power. I knew this organization helps hundreds of people and I wanted that to continue. So once again, I chose the path of forgiveness and acceptance. My ordination celebration still occurred and my supervisors still came and celebrated the call to ministry. Nevertheless, the mixed messages sent by this organization left me confused.

Churches everywhere leave these kinds of confusing messages all the time. This was a part of my awakening to how the disabled feel like second-class citizens in churches.

PITY AND PATERNALISM

Instead of empowering the disabled, many churches follow society's approach of pity and paternalism.[20] This means that many look at the disabled as objects of sorrow and targets of charity, rather than as complete humans with the potential to participate fully in the life of the church body. It is the opposite of empowerment. It keeps the disabled as recipients of charity instead of co-laborers in the work. It keeps the non-disabled as the ones with all the power who get to decide how to express kindness to the disabled.

A lot of disabled people have felt this pity and paternalism from the church first hand. For example, a church body might be motivated to raise money to bring meals to shut-ins at Christmas time. But that same church refuses to inconvenience itself so that the same shut-in can actually visit the church building on Sunday morning.

Paternalism can lead to a surprising kind of discrimination: hero worship. This is when a disabled leader is thought of as an extraordinary person by the church. His testimony is thrilling because it highlights the extreme obstacles he has had to overcome. But as strange as this may sound, this type of hero worship is actually detrimental. It dehumanizes rather than humanizes us.

You see, many disabled people want to blend into a community as regular humans. They don't want to be thought of as amazing or incredible. When people perceive you as amazing and incredible, it can be a subtle way of dehumanizing you so that you become somehow less than a complete human. You become a semi-human hero, and we all know that no human is a real hero. Heroes are two dimensional, but humans are multi-dimensional.

I know this criticism sounds strange, but hero worship has a way of keeping you in a special category in peoples' minds, which in turn makes people treat you differently. You might think, "yeah, but isn't it a 'good' kind of 'different'?" But how does "different" help include a disabled person who mainly desires to feel included?

Let me share some experiences with hero worship that still bring me anger and sadness. Many times as I am serving the Lord in the church nursery for example, I am told, "you are simply amazing"! When I ask why, they tell me things like, "because you are out helping so many when you deserve the help yourself." Why does this kind sentiment bring anger and sadness to mind? Mainly because it exposes how confused people still are about a disabled person's abilities. You see, when I have served as a nursery worker, I've done it just like anyone else does. I still smile when people walk in and while 3 babies cry at once. When it gets stressful, I stop and pray, and count the minutes until parents come back just like you might. Nothing amazing has happened. So why, just because I am serving God in a way similar to how anyone else would, do some people consider me "amazing"? I have often wanted to write a sermon on this, but I haven't yet because I still have so much frustration toward these individuals. The frustration is still strong even though I know these are people who mean well.

Think of the hurt this type of hero worship can promote in all kinds of people, not just those who are disabled. For example, hero worship has impacted my husband Ken. Whenever we are in a new environment, people praise him frequently for his loyalty to me even though I am disabled. They usually whisper the word disabled when they say this, probably because they hope my partial deafness will prevent me from hearing them. So, even though Ken and I complement one another in our marriage in a reciprocal way, why do these people consider him to be the hero in our relationship? It is so misleading to imagine us this way. Ken gets thoroughly annoyed by people who think he is in this marriage just to get brownie points. This is a lot of pressure on him and it creates tension between us even though we try to laugh over it.

Now, when a couple is newly affected by a disability, the non-disabled spouse may appreciate this hero worship praise at first during the adjustment period. But the non-disabled spouse needs to understand that God did not intend for us to become heroes. Instead, He intended us to become "Jesus with skin on" in our marriage relationships. This is God's calling for both partners in all Christian marriages. This means that the non-disabled spouse needs to respect the vows of marriage to stand by the disabled spouse in health and in sickness.

My middle son Chris has also been negatively impacted by hero worship. Chris happened to be the only one of our three kids not affected by a disability. For many years, he felt cheated because he felt a bit like he was missing out on what the rest of us were experiencing. We just kind of chuckled and loved him all the more. But when he became a teenager, many people began to bestow lofty qualities to Chris since he had to live with a family so affected by disabilities. This confused Chris to say the least. He genuinely hated the implication that his family was different or "less than" others in some way.

Like any teenager, Chris sometimes got angry with his parents' rules that limited his video game playing. Sometime he was annoyed with what we would serve for supper. And like most teens, his parents were not always his favorite people, especially in his late teen years. In those years, part of him looked for positive influences and examples from people outside the family. But the fact that some of us in the family are blind and others of us have different limitations was never something Chris felt bad about. He hated being put in this awkward position of being considered the hero in the family, even though it was usually well-meaning church people who put him in it. He often recounts how they just did not want to listen to his more positive version of our family life. For whatever reason, they just felt he must have a terrible life. Eventually, he has been able to turn this hero worship around and come to a more positive outlook now that he is in his twenties.

The moral of these stories is to make sure that if there is hero worship going on in your church, Jesus is the only hero!

Paternalism can show up in other some pretty sneaky ways. Joseph Shapiro tells an interesting story about it occurring at a memorial service.[21] The recently deceased had lived with a handicap, and comment after comment was made by those paying their respects that this person was inspiring due to his courageous attitude of living with the handicap. This was all well and good, but the final comment by the well-meaning pastor demonstrated his paternalism. He said that this person was the "least disabled person I have ever seen."[22] While this comment was obviously meant to be complimentary and came from a well-intended heart, it was still a hard-to-perceive form of discrimination. How so? It held up "least disabled" as the ideal, as something to be admired. The unspoken but logical converse of this is that the man's disability was worthy of disdain. Rather than simply accepting the man's disability as a part of his identity, it subtly reduces the deceased's value as a disabled person.

I hope you don't accuse me of just splitting hairs here. But think about it: if you were officiating at an African American person's funeral, would you say: "he was the least black person I have ever seen"? Of course not! His "blackness" is an important element of his identity and not something to be minimized. The same is true for those with disabilities.

In the end, discrimination by the church, both overt and subtle, has led many disabled people to halt their attempts to participate. This perpetuates a vicious cycle because once the disabled feel excluded, they will exclude the church as an option. Many disabled have come to see church as a "city on a hill." Jesus' metaphor is normally taken to be positive. But for the disabled, the "hill" imagery expresses the physical inaccessibility and socially inhospitable environment that can be the church.[23]

WE ALREADY FACE DISCRIMINATION IN THE WORLD

What is especially heartbreaking about discrimination by the church is that the disabled already face discrimination in the world. Whether it is inaccessible public buildings, schools that don't know how to accommodate different learning approaches, or companies with inequitable hiring practices, we face discrimination every single day.

What's more, many disabled people feel excluded from our own families and neighborhoods. Yes, as awful as it sounds, there are family members who outright belittle us and demean us for being disabled. Some disabled even become targets of abuse, simply because they're vulnerable and have difficulty defending themselves.

Plenty of disabled people have been forgotten or outright abandoned by their relatives. One extreme example of abuse that happened as recently as 2015 is a case in which a mother's boyfriend put vodka in the feeding tube of her developmentally delayed child, with this mother's consent. The case was never brought to trial, because the judge explained that the boy's life would not have amounted to much. I am just heartsick for this child of God. And even though I completely disagree with the way in which he was abused, I am also heartsick for his mother.

Both are beloved by our Savior. The mother was deeply in need of help, of some sort of intervention before her stress response occurred. I am committed, and I would hope churches would be committed as well, to walking beside those like this mother who felt the strains of parenthood. I am committed to offering other alternatives to people in similar situation.

More commonly, our disabilities can make it hard even to visit our families in the first place. As I am sure you can imagine, it can be a major event just to get out of our homes to connect with a loved one face-to-face. Visits can take huge amounts of time and energy to plan and coordinate, leaving us exhausted before we've even started to leave the house. And of course, there are some of us who can't leave the house at all.

Connecting with neighbors isn't a simple matter either. First of all, many of us don't have the mobility to move easily around the streets, even locally. And how are we supposed to connect with a neighbor who already feels scared and self-conscious about interacting with someone who is different? For a lot of us, it is just easier to stay inside and not make the effort to be involved in the local community.

All of this can cause us to feel isolated from regular life. It frequently causes us to feel despondent. Is it any surprise that depression rates are so high among the disabled?[24] Is it any surprise that we feel exhausted a lot of the time, not only in our bodies, but also in our minds, emotions and very souls? Is it any wonder that a lot of us don't have energy left over to engage a local church community like a non-disabled person might?

Would you believe that we even face discrimination from the medical establishment? I know you're probably thinking that I'm imagining things. But it's true. The medical profession, which has in so many ways drastically improved the lives of disabled people, has also in subtle ways promoted discrimination that makes us feel less than our full dignity and worth. How could this be possible?

You see, in spite of all the quality care given to the disabled by the medical community, the medical model's philosophy, goals and assessments of what constitute "health" do not necessarily take into account overall quality of life. For a person with disabilities, this oversight can actually threaten quality of life. What do I mean by this? Well, physicians commit to making a person healthy, which is a worthy goal. But most physicians look at disabilities as a sign of a physical infirmity. They keep striving through research to "fix" the disability. Many doctors attempt to bring the body of a disabled person closer to a more "normal" body. These are usually valiant efforts. But these doctors rarely discuss the patients' overall quality of life. They rarely ask their patients about their individual preferences. They rarely take into account their patients' levels of satisfaction.

What is the result? To begin with, I'm sure you can predict how this approach might increase stress and frustration for a person with a disability. For example, a friend of mine, an amputee, had this recent experience. He had a common cold. He went to the doctor for treatment, but instead he was bombarded with questions related to his missing limb. The illness itself hardly surfaced as a topic of conversation, even though that was why this friend had visited the doctor in the first place. My friend walked out of that doctor's office more stressed and further from treatment than when he went in. This sort of thing happens all the time in the life of disabled people.

Another relic from the medical model is a willingness to end life without medical intervention because the ill person is thought to be less able to live well due to the lack of a particular ability. There are still cases all over the world in which disabled infants are put to death or left to starve. There are cases in which a disabled person is forced to be homeless and beg. Disabilities happen due to some inadequacy in people, but this does not measure their life as less important than others. As I mentioned before, Jesus loved everybody, and He exhorts us to give more attention to the weaker among us. Let's not stand by and judge those who are living with a disability. Let's not judge their family members. But instead let's love on them in a way that normalizes the effects of the disability.

Another real-life example of the shortcomings of this medical model is the story of another friend of mine. This young woman was diagnosed with Sticklers Syndrome, which adversely affects many organs of the body, including the eyes. After many interventions and treatments for this condition, this woman chose not to have any more retina surgeries and instead go blind completely. Her decision was based on the fact that the restored vision would not be enough to function as a sighted person. This woman would also be hampered by all the restrictions from the final surgery—restrictions that would be life-long. For example, she would be unable to play sports and would have to avoid all heavy lifting. So, these restrictions would greatly reduce her ability to enjoy life, even though they could never stop a simple cough or sneeze. The drawbacks simply outweighed the benefits.

In response to her choice to stop treatment, my friend was told by a medical doctor that she had chosen to end her life and that she may as well just go home and stay there, isolated from the world. She was told she would never function as a normal person and that she would be a burden. But five years later, this same woman is a thriving member of her family and community. In spite of her poor treatment by the doctor under the influence of the medical model, this woman is happy. She contributes back to society.

This friend has become a strong advocate for the idea of

patient choice. She helps disabled people understand that though the judgments by these doctors may be painful, they are made out of ignorance. She educates people that though these doctors are well meaning, they do not always have a person's quality of life uppermost in their minds.

As you can see, one person's idea of a positive quality of life may differ shockingly from another's perception of how life's goals ought to be accomplished. Stanley Hauerwas, a Christian theologian and a medical doctor, has sought to bridge this gap between the medical model and the real lives of the disabled. He writes that a disabled person's life must be looked upon as an individualized plan from God rather than as a medical abnormality.[25] This plan must be carried out according to the individual leading of the Spirit, rather than according to the medical model's universal prescription for health. In other words, medical treatments for people with disabilities ought to take into account God's individual plans without chaining all patients to the exact same standard.

So you see, we face discrimination in every part of life, even from the medical profession—the very profession that nobly attempts to help us. We face it at work, on the streets of our neighborhoods, and from our own families. So, many of us end our weeks exhausted from the daily battering of discrimination in the regular world. Like so many other people, we hope that the church experience will lift our spirits and renew our resolution to face a new week of challenge and hardship. Despite all the negative encounters of discrimination against the disabled, we hold this hope that at church at least we will taste God's love coming through His people.

But instead, many of us only encounter more discrimination when we get to church.

WHY DISCRIMINATION IN THE CHURCH?

Why do churches discriminate against the disabled? One of the main reasons for it seems to be a historical association between sin and disability. Disability has often been seen as representative of sin's presence. In other words, sin has been considered the cause of disability. So, instead of sharing grace with the disabled, churches have sometimes shunned people because of this alleged sign of transgression. This perspective has left many disabled people hurt and ashamed.

I have several friends who have been to churches where people tell them that they need to have more faith in order to be healed of their disabilities. This belief makes disabled people feel as if there is something defective in their faith. For example, one friend of mine shared with me about how every time she went to a Bible study, the group automatically prayed for her blindness to be corrected. This woman was comfortable with her blindness and it was becoming frustrating to explain this to the other Bible study members. She eventually asked them to stop praying for her healing. But this inspired ridicule and the blind woman eventually stopped attending all church activities.

Others I know have been told that they continue to struggle with a disability because they haven't adequately repented from a particular sin. While there are a few examples of people in Scripture whose sin did lead to a physical ailment, it would contradict Jesus' teaching to say that all disability is a direct result of a person's sin.

Jesus dealt pretty directly with this notion when He healed the man born blind in John 9. "His disciples asked him, 'Rabbi, who sinned, this man, or his parents, that he was born blind?'" (vs. 2, NIV). It is not surprising that the disciples would ask this. They had some Old Testament examples to choose from in which a person's illness or physical challenge really did result from some disobedience to God. For instance, when Miriam opposed her brother Moses' unquestioned authority as God's mouthpiece, God struck her with leprosy (Numbers 12). Wouldn't it be natural to conclude, as most Jews did in those days, that *all* ailments and physical difficulties were the result of sin, as Miriam's had been?

But Jesus revealed that many physical limits can have a much more gracious cause than mere sin. He responded to His disciples: "'Neither this man nor his parents sinned,' said Jesus, 'but this happened so that the works of God might be displayed in him'" (vs. 3). Other than in the few cases when Scripture clearly identifies a disability as a direct result of a person's sin, how can any of us truly know the cause? And if we could know the cause, why would it matter? Jesus had an attitude of compassion for all the disabled people He encountered, and He sought to touch them with healing and with the love of God. He did this whatever the source of the physical challenge. Jesus continued His explanation to the disciples:

> *"As long as it is day, we must do the works of him who sent me. Night is coming, when no one can work. While I am in the world, I am the light of the world."*
>
> *After saying this, he spit on the ground, made some mud with the saliva, and put it on the man's eyes. "Go," he told him, "wash in the Pool of Siloam," … So the man went and washed, and came home seeing* (vs. 4-7, NIV).

If Jesus could have this redemptive attitude toward the source of peoples' disabilities, why can't everyone in His church? Even if most churches these days don't overtly teach that all disabilities are caused by sin, why do so many in the church still hesitate to engage people with disabilities, as if they might taint themselves with the brokenness of the world?

Part of the answer, just plain and simple, is ignorance and fear. One friend of mine described her treatment by her local church: "I know Jesus and His love. [But] every time I try to involve myself into a worship service or Bible study … I am reminded that I am defective. Some church leaders have even asked me to leave the activity. When I have questioned them on why I have to leave … I have heard that my deformed eyes are evil and very uncomfortable. I am so afraid of getting hurt again." When it came down to it, this woman's different appearing eyes (something quite common for the those who are blind), made people in her church uncomfortable.

If you bought this book and have gotten this far reading it, I doubt that you knowingly hold to or teach a viewpoint like this. But still it lurks in the background of church history and it lurks in some churches even today. It haunts us all rather than helps us.

Because of stories like the ones in this chapter, and hundreds more like them that I could tell you, I want to help the disabled realize their full potential in the Body of Christ. I want to walk beside local churches to help them welcome the disabled. I want to provide encouragement for the disabled and for churches to overcome these narratives and to follow Jesus' command to invite all to the Great Banquet.

Chapter Four
Sawubona

Before I get into all the practical elements of disability ministry, I want to tell you some stories from my Doctor of Ministry project. I wrote my doctoral thesis around an experiment I conducted on intentional Christian community. I created a virtual, on-line, intentional community for the disabled. You need to hear some of the stories of this community because they will give you an insider's view of how the disabled struggle with church. But best of all, these stories will give you a taste of what God's community *could* be and how you could be a part of it.

The idea of intentional Christian communities goes way back, almost to the beginning of the church. You might even call the primitive church in the Book of Acts an intentional community. I found that when a community is intentional, it opens the way to include the disabled. So, I did a lot of research on the topic and I tried to use as many elements of traditional, intentional communities as I could when I created this community.

It fascinated me to learn how to make an intentional community out of a *virtual* community. Several books have been published about intentional virtual communities,[26] so I drew heavily on those for the "how to." Virtual communities have the advantage of giving a voice to the voiceless because everyone can say something and be heard through digitalized access. As you can imagine, having a voice is one of the biggest needs of the disabled. Besides, it meant that we didn't have to leave our homes, which, as I've already mentioned, is a big deal for many of us disabled.

I wanted to accomplish two things through this community. First, I wanted to use good research methods to find out more objectively why so many disabled people do not participate in local churches. Second, I wanted to teach fellow disabled believers the privileges and responsibilities of being God's people. I wanted to find out if I could activate them into fuller church participation if I created this community that met their needs at their own level.

I began by picking a name for this community. I decided to call it "Sawubona." Sawubona is a Zulu greeting that loosely means, "I *see* you, and I *want* to be in your presence."[27] This greeting expresses the idea that "I acknowledges all of your strengths and weaknesses, your good parts and bad, and I still choose to accept you." When we greet each other this way, we recognize that, even though we can plainly see each other's shortcomings, we embrace each other as friends anyway. We agree to accept all aspects of each other, including a possible disability. The term is a mutual invitation to be in one another's presence, in spite of, or even because of, the other person's needs. It means to be fully in the presence of the other, despite distractions and other challenges to the friendship.

I thought this was an appropriate term to describe the kind of community disabled people need in order to achieve fuller church participation. The concept establishes a sense of mutual respect and cooperation between the disabled and the church.

The intentional community ended up with seven participants,

including me. That might not sound like a lot to you, but the small size gave us a very high quality of interaction. Over 200 people applied to join the group. These people came forward after just a few days of advertising my research project. This is an excellent response as far as research goes. And many others besides let me know about their interest in one way or another. Now, I am pointing this out to let you know about the overwhelming desire of the disabled to participate in church related activities. So, use this enthusiasm to your church's advantage. More importantly, use this enthusiasm to grow and strengthen the Kingdom of God.

But despite this overwhelming response, I knew I wanted to keep it small. So, I picked only the first six who got their application paperwork in to me.

Through no design of my own, the group ended up being composed of all women, most of us middle-aged. I didn't know the identity or the disability of any of the other six participants when we started out. But completely by coincidence, all of us shared some degree of blindness and some degree of hearing impairment. Also, one of us was a quadriplegic (limited use of all four limbs) and another was a paraplegic (limited use of two limbs). All of us were professing Christians.

We "spoke" together daily. I say this in quotations because each of us had to use special voice-to-text software to communicate. In order to make our communication more smooth, we also used Skype, chat rooms and other methods to stay connected electronically. All this helped us interact directly with one another, which was especially important given how spread out we were. Four of us were in Minnesota, where I was living at the time; one of us was in Oregon, one in Washington State, and one in Ohio.

Each of our almost daily discussions revolved around a specific topic. Every week I'd post one of my journal entries.

Each entry involved a topic like: "the hassles of being disabled," "living a radical life for Jesus," "acceptance versus exclusion," and "learning from the Scriptures how God wants disabled individuals to interact with others." I'd pose all kinds of questions about what it was like to live with a disability, and what it was like to be disabled while trying to connect with a church. Each journal entry launched dozens and dozens of email discussions between group members every week. This virtual community was also an avenue for prayer requests and praise reports, which we had a lot of, as you'll see in a moment.

We ended up with thousands of pieces of electronic communication. The community formally existed for 11 weeks back in the summer and fall of 2011. I interviewed everybody before and after the 11 weeks in the hope of getting a "before and after" snapshot.

A lot of amazing fruit came out of this project. We got to network with each other. We came to empathize with one another and with the challenges that each of us face. One amazing thing that happened was that each member expressed a desire to lead a Bible study within our Sawubona community. It was fantastic because I saw this as an opportunity to train everybody in leadership, self-assertiveness, and Bible study skills. So we each took a favorite passage from Scripture and led a fruitful discussion for a week at a time. It was a great way to help each other with leadership styles and with Bible study tools and resources. It gave us a chance to try out alternative formats such as Braille and audio. It also let us experiment with new technology applications that bridge gaps for us. For instance, some of used new tools provided by Bible Gateway, along with many other programs like that.

Best of all, almost everybody reported an increase in their church-related activities as a result of our time together. Almost all of us reported an improved level of acceptance by a local church. I was thrilled. Let me tell you a little bit about how we got there.

A lot of these stories from Sawubona are organized around themes that kept coming up in our discussions. These were themes like, "identity in Christ versus identity in the world," "making our voices heard," "spiritual gifts," "taking ownership," "self-advocacy," "engaging the local church" and "strategies for reconciliation."

THEME #1: IDENTITY IN CHRIST VS. IDENTITY IN THE WORLD

Probably the most foundational way I hoped to impact the group participants was to help them think differently about their identities. Many disabled people do not understand their new identity in Christ. This contributes to their feeling of being second-class citizens at church. In the world we might be known as "that disabled person down the street" or "the person with special needs at my office." But many don't realize that because of their faith in Jesus they have a new identity that transcends their disability. The church is supposed to be the place where this new identity is re-affirmed and strengthened so that it gradually comes to dominate a person's self-narrative. But sadly, church is often a place where we continue to be known as "that disabled person in the other pew." Often, our worldly identity gets reinforced at church.

So, first I asked everybody to examine the ways they refer to themselves. I wanted people to become aware of when they called themselves things like, "the blind woman" or "a person who uses a wheelchair" as their primary self-identification.

This idea was greeted with a lot of enthusiasm, since everyone agreed that it was easy to slip into thinking of oneself primarily according to a disability diagnosis.

Then as the group members became more self-aware of how they referenced themselves, I encouraged them to start using language that spoke of their spiritual identity instead. This includes using titles such as "daughter of the king" or "sister of Christ." I directed them to lots of Bible passages like 2 Corinthians 5:17: "If anyone is in Christ, that person is a new creation; the old has gone, the new is here!" (NIV). Ephesians 1 became a big reference point in the group, with its identity descriptors like "blessed" (vs. 3), chosen (vs. 4), "holy and blameless" (vs. 4), adopted (vs. 5) redeemed (vs. 7), and lavished with the riches of God's grace (vv. 7-8)(NIV). I wanted the participants to get used to thinking of themselves with this biblical language instead of using purely physical descriptions and markers. As our time together rolled on, people started reporting the powerful effect of thinking of themselves in these new ways.

I felt this process was really foundational to everything else that I hoped would be accomplished in the community. If people can start to see themselves as God sees them, then I think there is a stronger possibility that they'll be able to do some of the other brave and adventurous things that I believe Jesus encourages the disabled to do.

THEME #2: MAKING OUR VOICES HEARD

The members of Sawubona daily expressed their desire for a voice. As I've talked about already, the disabled often feel as if their voices are not being heard. Some of us are literally voiceless. Even when we're not, many of us struggle with communication barriers of all kinds.

Let me give you an example of how communication struggles

affect daily life. Let's take something that a lot of us take for granted: transportation. For you, transportation might be a simple matter of hoping in your car, jumping on the bus or pulling out your bike. But as you can imagine, it isn't so simple for us.

Much of the problem begins with the fact that many of us are homebound. The very nature of being homebound hinders our access to the same sort of communication options of non-disabled people. You won't see us strolling through the park or down the street as often as you'll see your non-disabled neighbors. Even if we aren't homebound, you still won't see us out and about as much as others. And even if you do see us out regularly, our attention will probably be directed toward navigating the environment more than interacting with neighbors. This means that our casual conversations become less casual. All this translates into social isolation and therefore voicelessness. We won't hear as much of the neighborly gossip or be able to share with you as much of the news from our lives.

And we can't just pop up to the store to grab a newspaper. Basic transportation is a huge barrier for most of us. In the city many disabled people take the bus and this helps with the smaller, more spontaneous trips. But in rural or even suburban areas transportation usually has to be arranged through volunteer driver programs. These programs often require reservations a week in advance. Furthermore, they typically match you up with a few other disabled people to be more efficient. You rarely know those other people and you don't have much control over when you get picked up or dropped off in their line up. This means you could be in the van or in the car for long periods of time before and after your destination. For example, if I arrange to go grocery shopping at the local Price Chopper, the ride is normally 20 minutes. But we often pick up someone else with disabilities and so the ride gets extended to an hour.

You are also restricted to a set amount of time at the store in order to insure the driver maintains his or her schedule. So if I meet a friend or see a bulletin that catches my interest I have a dilemma. I have to choose between getting all my items on my shopping list or talking to that friend or taking the time to find someone to read me the flyer.

Now, it's true that some of us drive. The Department of Transportation reported that "locally" 62% of the disabled "drove" a vehicle in comparison to 86% of nondisabled.[28] I was pleasantly surprised at how high the number was for the disabled when I discovered this. It means a higher degree of independence for more people. However, I want to point out that driving comes with its own set of variables. There can be a high cost for adaptive equipment for the car. There can also be limitations on a disabled person's license. For instance, some are only allowed to drive during the day and not on highways. Besides all this, there is usually a much higher cost to insure a disabled driver. So by making simple driving fairly restrictive for many of us, these variables tend to drown out the voices that are just trying to be heard.

You can see that even very simple tasks such as getting some milk and eggs can have many layers of extra consideration for a person with disabilities. Knowing this will help you to be more aware of what your church members with special needs go through daily. It is part of the reason most of us are so exhausted and have so little left in the tank by the time we reach Sunday morning.

I bring these points out to illustrate how our voices get taken away by things most of us would never even consider. All the extra layers increase our sense of voicelessness and social isolation. We might not have quick access to the news. We might not have the ability to be involved in public dialogue. If the

Internet is down one day or the power is out in our homes, it means we'll probably have no access to what's happening in the world or in the community, and we certainly won't have a way to respond.

Think about what all this does to our voice in politics. It is no simple matter for us to go to the local polling station during an election. Some polling places, especially the ones in churches, are simply physically inaccessible. How is a person supposed to make his voice heard with so many barriers in place?

The Sawubona community spent a lot of time talking about this issue of voicelessness. Each one of us could relate many stories of when our disabilities prevent us from being heard.

Probably the biggest thing that made our members feel voiceless was the perception of exclusion. All of us had experienced exclusion due to our disabilities. But for a person with disabilities, real exclusions can lead one to have an overall lens of exclusion for all of life. By this I mean that it can become easy to interpret everything as exclusion and rejection, even if it is not.

To begin to deal with this, I shared a journal entry early in the 11 weeks which talked about exclusion as a universal experience. This means that even the non-disabled feel excluded at times. The idea that everybody, disabled or not, encounters exclusion at one time or another, turned out to be a very freeing idea to Sawubona members. It gave us all a sense that our experience was normal.

For example, let's say two couples walk into a church sanctuary on Sunday morning. Neither couple has attended prior to this visit. One couple is shabbily dressed and has two fussy children. The other couple has more traditional Sunday attire and has warm smiles. The greeters meet the former couple with cold kindness and do not offer any extra words of encouragement.

The latter couple is warmly received and actually ushered to a pew to sit. When the first couple asks where they should sit, they are waved to a row in the back.

I didn't make this up. This example actually happened to some close friends. They were the couple that was enthusiastically welcomed. They felt helpless for this other couple and they decided to turn right around and leave. When they were leaving, the ushers asked if there was a problem. When they mentioned this exclusion of the other couple, it became awkward. Apologies were given and yet still no one reached out to welcome the other couple. My friends went ahead and left and they carried with them this burden of welcoming all to God's house.

This concept of the universality of exclusion interestingly led to a renewed interest in trying out church again. Some Sawubona members felt that if non-disabled people at times felt exclusion, then perhaps we shared a common experience. This meant that perhaps we could relate more easily with the non-disabled than we'd assumed. Perhaps association with a lot of non-disabled people at church didn't have to be such an alienating experience after all?

THEME #3: DISABLED PEOPLE HAVE SPIRITUAL GIFTS TOO

I big part of finding your voice is discovering your spiritual gifts. When a person knows her spiritual gifts, she better understands how to be involved in the church. Paul wrote to the Corinthians, "When you come together, *each of you* has a hymn, or a word of instruction, a revelation, a tongue or an interpretation" (1 Cor. 14:26, NIV). In other words, everyone is contributing to the corporate life in one way or another. But did you know that many disabled people feel as if they don't have any gifts, or that their gifts don't matter? It is easy to see why so many feel this way, just from the stories I've already told you. Would you want to stick your neck out and contribute to the church if you got shot down, dismissed or ignored every time? Would you want to contribute if it takes lots of effort to make that contribution—effort that most others don't notice or appreciate?

I thought Sawubona was the perfect opportunity to talk about the good news that "each of us" has spiritual gifts, and that our gifts are just as important as everybody else's, because each plays a part, "so that the church may be built up" (vs. 26b). So, early in our time together I surveyed the participants to discover their spiritual gifts. We explored our gifts and discussed them. We talked a lot about how these gifts reflected our spiritual identity versus our worldly identity.

We talked quite a bit about the pay off of contributing to community. All the members had stories of previous times in their lives when they were involved in various communities and the difference they'd felt as contributors, "so that the church may be built up." For example, one participant described a previous community in which she was the main cook. But due to her blindness, she was unable to drive. In this community, this inability to drive was not a hindrance. In fact, it allowed another person to share his gift of stewardship through shopping. So, being the cook and sharing the shopping duties with another had reduced her self-consciousness about what she could not do. But later, when she lived outside of that community, she was constantly reminded of what she could not do, instead of how she had contributed.

Over the course of the 11 weeks, every member of Sawubona came to feel more in touch with their spiritual gifts. We all gained a renewed appreciation of the importance and power of our gifts. Everyone felt an increased sense of responsibility to use those gifts to benefit God's community.

THEME #4: TAKING OWNERSHIP AND SELF-ADVOCACY

We spent a lot of time discussing my teaching about biblical responsibilities. One of my main goals for doing this virtual community was to help the participants learn to take ownership of their responsibilities to God's community.

Many people with disabilities struggle to sing in a choir or teach a Sunday school class. But I encouraged them all to begin taking ownership of their responsibilities in Christ by finding a specific topic or passage from the Bible and leading a study on this topic. Everyone seemed very eager to do this. All of the group members reported that they'd been rejected from teaching in the past by churches because of their disabilities. So we all took turns leading a different Bible study. And I have to say that everyone proved quite capable. I was a little surprised that most people did not do a study about disabilities. Instead, most did a study about God's love and wisdom.

One of the biggest barriers Sawubona members needed to overcome was the sense that churches rejected them because they were perceived as unreliable. Several members talked about how their physical limitations led them to change their schedules at the last moment, sometimes without notice. As a result of this, several of us felt that people at churches were reluctant to rely on us.

This barrier led to some great problem solving by our group. We trouble shot each person's anxiety about being perceived as unreliable and we came up with some fantastic solutions for each other so that we could still meet our obligations. Here are some solutions that seemed promising. We decided that if you are scheduled to teach or in some way lead a group, and you are concerned about being unable to follow through, you should have a back up plan. Maybe your volunteer driver has an emergency that day. Maybe you are simply unwell or otherwise physically unable the lead that day. You can ask someone else you've already picked out to sub for you. This should be someone with whom you can discuss the back up plan ahead of time, someone to whom you can supply your notes and preparation materials. You can also try to find a driver from a pool of people whom you know will already be attending.

To you, the reader, these solutions might seem like such minor problems. But just having permission to talk about a possible problem is so freeing for us. It is freeing because we often think we're not allowed to discuss these simple arrangements. Whether or not the feeling is based on truth, it feels like most others don't always have to make these sort of back up plans. You know that phrase, to "talk about the elephant in the room"? Well, we often think we're not allowed to talk about this kind of "elephant" because most of you don't need to. But it helps us when we can talk about it.

By talking through this particular barrier in Sawubona, two good things were accomplished. First, we all gained a lot of wisdom about how to take ownership of our duties. If we were really going to contribute to the church we needed to learn how to balance our responsibilities to the community with our needs and limitations. The discussion helped us all to discover this balance more effectively. The other good outcome was that all the group members reported by the end of Sawubona that they felt more accepted by their local churches. Some of this sense of acceptance may have come from their improved ways of coping with responsibilities. It may also have come from just renewed confidence in their own abilities to navigate and balance duty with needs.

THEME #5: ENGAGING THE LOCAL CHURCH

This experience of a virtual community did carry over to help the participants in the non-disabled world, just like I hoped.

Mainly, it helped us coach one other to communicate with our local churches about our particular needs and gifts.

At first, we spent a lot of our time together answering my questions about why some of us didn't go to church or why we went to church infrequently. We heard lots of stories from each other about how we felt reluctant to be involved in a local church because of the various barriers, exclusions and rejections we'd all encountered. One member even held an official leadership position in her church. But she felt increasingly reluctant to attend because of the barriers she regularly experienced.

A lot of this sense of exclusion came from the physical inaccessibility of a particular part of the sanctuary or worship service. For example, three members explained how they could not physically get to the choir loft. Two members shared how they could physically get to the loft, but the choir leader feared for their safety and refused to let them participate.

Another example of inaccessibility was communion. All participants were physically able to partake in communion. Nevertheless, four participants had experienced rejection during the Lord's Supper. One told us of how her pastor used a silent means of indicating when to take the bread and wine. But this didn't help my friend because she was partially blind. The pastor did not want the disabled person to receive a verbal prompting because he thought it would cause disruption. Two other members explained how the deacons refused to allow them to partake in communion because they were afraid the elements would get dropped, even those these two were able to pass the elements of communion.

These conversations eventually led to discussions about how we might overcome our barriers so we could participate more in church. We brainstormed possible resolutions so we could effectively re-engage. One of the great things about doing this as a group was that we were able to swap advice and wisdom about what to do. We discovered that we all needed one another in order to make progress.

I also found it necessary to help the members think differently in regard to what makes up a church family. We talked a lot about church being a family rather than a location to visit. To help with this, I borrowed a few ideas from a movement called "new monasticism."[29] This got us to think of the local church in a broader way. For instance, a local church can include home churches in which participants meet in one another's homes. This redefinition of church was necessary, since the expanded understanding helped members of Sawubona open their hearts once again to the possibility that they could relate positively to a church.

Each Sawubona member chose to work on improving her attendance at a local church. We each picked some goals to help us make the improvements. Then we monitored one another's progress toward those goals and prayed for one another along the way. During this time, we re-examined the various barriers to attendance in order to find ways to overcome them. Some members even acknowledged that not all church activities would work for all people, including the disabled. Rather than choosing bitterness over this fact, it gave most of us a sense of relief.

Eventually, we shared the results and we celebrated our triumphs that came from these improvements. Probably my greatest joy from Sawubona was that everybody's participation in church increased over the course of our time together. The people who had been least involved in church prior to Sawubona had increased their involvement more than anyone. Each person reported specific ways she was now more active at church.

For example, one person had started to attend a Bible study that helped her overcome her perceived exclusion. She had advocated for herself so that it now met at a time that was more conducive to her health limitations. This group also allowed her to conference call into the group when she was unable to attend physically.

Another member started teaching a Sunday School class for preschoolers. She had always wanted to do this but the church had refused her past offers. She didn't question their refusal. But this time she approached the church's Christian education director and shared her interest. The director seemed hesitant. This lady acknowledged this hesitation and invited the director to ask her questions. She invited questions about her background, about her understanding of the Bible and any other topics, including questions about her disabilities. This member openly answered everything she could. She is now teaching for a second year. She also started making homemade items to put into prayer baskets.

A third member reported that she began to ease into church by attending a fellowship meal after a church service held at a local restaurant. She had so many positive interactions with people at this fellowship meal that she started to attend the Sunday worship service regularly.

Someone else in Sawubona wanted to work in the nursery. She was told that she was not qualified. She immediately became defensive. In the past, before getting involved in Sawubona, she allowed this defensiveness to stop her from either gaining skills or finding another ministry. But this time, she approached the nursery coordinator with a different tactic. The coordinator gave the same response of "no." But, with the encouragement of the other Sawubona members, she responded by asking some simple, non-defensive questions. These questions led to a healthy and meaningful dialogue. It turns out that the coordinator had concerns about how this person would determine where a baby was in the room. Our Sawubona member explained her various coping mechanisms for such things. This satisfied any doubt on the coordinator's part, and this woman started helping in the nursery. Not surprisingly, her involvement in the nursery further led her to meet more new people, which in turn led her to cultivate lots more relationships. These relationships further strengthened this woman's sense of acceptance.

One woman shared how she decided to become a greeter on Sunday mornings. This put her in a position to come in contact with many attendees in a natural, unforced way. This boosted her sense of belonging. This experience encouraged her to begin reading Scripture as a part of the service. The church warmly received this gift of Scripture reading. She used her Braille note taker to access Scriptures, which provided a natural way for her to educate the church about accommodations that blind people may need. This lady wrote: "I am thrilled and blessed to know I am not only a child of God, but a member of a church family here on earth."

Do you remember my earlier story in Chapter Two about a friend whose Bible study members kept praying for her to be healed of blindness? Well, she was a Sawubona participant. With everyone's encouragement, she re-approached this same Bible class during the Sawubona community. This time, when they prayed for her healing, she thanked each member. She also asked if anyone had questions about her blindness. Many questions surfaced and she answered willingly. She reported that for the next few weeks, they still prayed for her healing. She then reported that the healing prayers gradually ceased and they started praying for other needs in her life—needs that she actually felt and which she wanted them to pray about. She believes this choice to react positively allowed a healthy dialogue to occur. The members of the Bible study started to get to know her on a personal level and could then pray more specifically and more compassionately.

By the end of Sawubona, all our members reported an increasing sense of acceptance at their local church. This level of acceptance didn't always correlate to an increase in participation. But acceptance is a necessary foundation if we hope to improve participation in any way.

THEME #6: STRATEGIES FOR RECONCILIATION

Much of our connection, especially toward the end, came from talking about practical strategies for both churches and the disabled to reconcile with each other. As I mentioned above, reconciliation was my ultimate aim. I don't need to repeat how so many disabled people feel alienated from church. As you already know, I think this is a situation that needs to change. So I heavily emphasized reconciliation to the Sawubona community.

RECONCILIATION STEP ONE: EXPRESSING HURTS

I started by providing an avenue to express hurts. I'm sure I don't need to tell you that perceived hurts need to be worked through in order to open up a pathway for reconciliation. If a person feels like his hurts and grievances never get addressed, then you might as well give up on true reconciliation. If you felt as if your enemy were an ongoing threat to you, you wouldn't be open to reconciling. And if your enemy started making overtures of friendship, you wouldn't believe them if you hadn't first dealt with the causes of the past conflicts. If you don't deal with past hurts, you probably won't be open to renewed friendship no matter how hard the other party works at reconciliation.

So many Sawubona forums became times of sharing our hurts with one another. I'll spare you the many stories, but this was a necessary step for the members to take. It is also a necessary step for disabled people in your congregation, or for disabled people you hope to reach, if there is hope for reconciliation. These weren't just gripe sessions: they were doorways to health.

RECONCILIATION STEP TWO:
DISCERNING "REAL" VERSUS "PERCEIVED" HURTS

A second stage of reconciliation after acknowledging hurts is to tease out the difference between real and perceived hurts. This is really tricky work and it took a heavy investment of time and effort from everyone in Sawubona to get through it. If we'd been too quick to dismiss someone's hurt as only perceived, we would have lost their trust in the rest of us and we possibly would have lost their participation altogether. As I'm sure you know, the pain from a perceived offense can be just as awful as the pain from a real offense. It can be really hard to tell the difference. While we were working through this, the length of our emails grew and became more frequent as we each tried to help one another carefully sort through the facts and the emotions.

In one example, a member shared how she felt isolated at church due to her inability to make eye contact. After a lot of listening, different members gently challenged her to evaluate the times she felt isolated. They wanted her to discover if she played a role in this isolation, even if had been a small role. So we asked her things like, "do you sit alone or do you try to engage others in conversation?" After much reflection on this situation, this person discovered her feelings of isolation were real. The group validated her feeling of rejection. We took it one step further and encouraged her to find proactive ways to counteract the isolation, such as saying hello to three people on a Sunday morning.

Through this kind of slow and careful group discernment,

other members found that some of their offenses and hurts were more perceived than real. Because of the loving and accepting environment that we'd established in Sawubona, everyone became comfortable challenging the perceptions of other members. At times we openly disagreed with each other about the possible causes of barriers we'd encountered.

We eventually came up with a set of criteria to tell the difference between real and perceived barriers. We came to define a barrier to be "real" when it created physical obstacles that a disabled person could not overcome, even after we'd attempted to adjust our own personal perceptions. Real barriers included inaccessible buildings, inaccessible reading materials, and inaccessible transportation. These were things that wouldn't change just by thinking about them differently.

Perceived barriers included a sense of being a second-class citizen, a feeling of being inadequate, and a feeling of being out of the ordinary. These were barriers that we could do something about, especially as we absorbed the teaching about our new identity in Christ.

One barrier we talked a lot about was "isolation." We found that isolation can be both real and perceived. We can isolate ourselves, and others can isolate us. For instance, we might retreat to the far corner of the church lobby in order to keep our distance from people in an effort to escape their rejection. This could make us feel isolated, even when we've contributed to the feeling. Or, other people could purposefully avoid us during the greeting time because we might obviously appear to be different. There is little we can do about it if someone is determined to avoid us. So when we feel isolated it gets trickier to figure out the difference between real and perceived exclusion.

The idea of "perceived vs. real" doesn't mean that the perceived barriers are fake or only in our heads. They still have the power to hinder the disabled from getting involved in church. But they are barriers that the disabled person has power to deal with effectively.

Here's the key: we demonstrated sincere empathy with each other's struggles. When someone feels sincere empathy, it creates a sense of safety. From this sense of safety, we can start to get unstuck. You know how this is, because everyone, whatever the level of ability, responds well to expressions of empathy. In our case, empathy provided us all with a safe foundation from which we could encourage one another to move outside our comfort zones.

And here's the big danger if don't express empathy for a person's struggles, real or perceived: disabled people will shut you out and you'll lose credibility in their eyes. In other words, don't go thinking that you will be able to pastor disabled people by telling them, "that barrier is just in your mind." That will be received as dismissive and it will erode the disabled person's trust in your leadership. If you are not disabled, you don't have the credibility to tell someone with disabilities that it's in his mind. Sawubona's discernment came because we already had credibility to speak on these matters to one another. The credibility we had with each other was amplified by an atmosphere of mutual consideration and love for one another. This atmosphere happened because each of us chose to be vulnerable and to share our personal struggles with the others. By hearing one another's stories, we all knew that everybody could identify deeply with everyone else.

All this to say, before you jump into discerning the difference between a disabled person's "real" and "perceived" hurts, work mostly on building trust and on creating a relationship of mutual love and consideration. You may never get to the discerning phase, but that is okay.

The slow process of deciphering between real and perceived offenses had a powerful effect. All of us ended up feeling as though we were more capable of figuring out the difference between the two by the end of Sawubona. This was very empowering to us. Another effect was that we all realized we bear some of the responsibility to improve our connection with local churches.

Most of the people in Sawubona also stated a desire to find a mentor who could help them continue to work through the emotions around feeling excluded and rejected. We took this as another sign that our group efforts were working, since it meant that people recognized their need to keep addressing issues that prevented reconciliation.

RECONCILIATION STEP THREE: DIALOGING WITH CHURCH LEADERSHIP

The third step of reconciliation was to make contact with church leadership. This means that disabled people need to make church leadership aware of the barriers that block their participation in church. In order for reconciliation to work, both the disabled and the church need to work together to establish an environment that brings glory to God. The disabled can't do all the work of reconciliation, or else it isn't real reconciliation. This starts with the disabled educating church leadership.

By the time I re-interviewed everyone at the end of our 11 weeks, each member of Sawubona indicated her desire to share some of her perceived exclusions with both church leadership and with other disabled people. This meant that our efforts as a group were working—the individual members showed more willingness to express and work through their hurts, and they were moving closer to re-establishing relationships with the church based on trust. Even though we all agreed that we were responsible for resolving our sense of perceived exclusions, we thought the willingness to share with church leaders was important because it might increase a church's overall culture of acceptance.

We talked about helpful strategies for approaching the leadership. One way to begin this is for both parties to acknowledge that acceptance of the other is the foundation of reconciliation. Remember, the word sawubona reflects the notion of a person truly seeing another person and then accepting the other. This acceptance needs to occur first in order to bring about reconciliation. Acceptance refrains from trying to fix a disability. Instead, it focuses on how this disability will fit in to the family of God.

Disabled people can show their acceptance of leaders by acknowledging that many church leaders sincerely want to include the disabled but simply lack language and resources to successfully assimilate them. If disabled people assume that church leadership purposefully and intentionally excludes them, then the leadership will be less open to work with them. It is hard for leaders to see someone as an ally if that person is constantly accusing them of wrongdoing or of bad motives.

When a foundation of mutual acceptance is established, church leadership and the disabled can begin to talk about practical ways to overcome barriers. In this discussion, church leadership needs to hold loosely their "sacred cows." For instance, a local church might find that a particular architectural configuration is very precious to them, even though it is inaccessible. Leadership needs to be willing to say, "this configuration, as precious as it is to us, isn't what's most important to the church. Let's be willing to figure out a way to change this so we can make the building more accessible to everyone."

On the other hand, the disabled need to acknowledge that

some accessibility changes might be downright too expensive and disruptive to make in the short term. The disabled person can still advocate for the change. But he needs to maintain patience when it seems that little progress is being made.

Both parties need to work at reconciliation. When we started to talk about this topic in Sawubona, I'd say that most of the comments were about how the church needs to do things differently to make reconciliation happen. But as the community matured, most of us acknowledged that we as disabled people play a critical role and that we need to offer love, acceptance and forgiveness as well.

In the next chapter I include a lot more of the practical steps to cultivate reconciliation between the disabled and churches. Reconciliation among God's people can happen when we express our hurts, when we differentiate between real and perceived hurts, and when we carry on proactive conversations with leadership about changing the real barriers.

An added benefit of Sawubona's structure was that we could regularly check in with each other to see how we were progressing in our efforts to overcome barriers. We held each other accountable to our commitments to make changes. Since we all trusted one another so much, this accountability worked well. I'm delighted to say that we all made progress with our various barriers.

Chapter Five
Some Strategies for Success

In the last chapter, I told you some stories from Sawubona because I wanted you to get a picture of the power of community in the lives of disabled believers. Community is a major part of God's means to empower His people. Community activates us to become fully devoted followers of Christ. Community heals the darkness of our hearts. Disabled people need community to do this for them no less than you need it. You could be a part of making this happen for many disabled people if you would learn to include them in your community.

If you're anything like me, you're thinking, "this is all very nice Theresa, but let's get on to some practical ways that I can improve the way we work with the disabled. Just how exactly am I supposed to include them in our community?" Here are a few practical suggestions for including the disabled.

LOOK AT THE DISABLED THROUGH GOD'S EYES

The biggest and most important strategy for successfully including the disabled is for you and your church to look at the disabled through God's eyes rather than through the world's. If you don't have this going for you, none of the other strategies I'm about to recommend will be of any help to you.

Most of us hold on to some false, underlying beliefs about disabled people. These beliefs can translate into unhelpful actions. For example, many of us look at disabled people as slightly less than fully human. Before you protest ("*We* don't do that at *our* church"), take a close look at your own perceptions and reactions to disabled people. In your mind, have you ever secretly downgraded what you thought a disabled person could accomplish because of his disability? Have you ever silently thought that the quality of a disabled person's relationship with God was less than yours? I'm not suggesting that you thought any of this maliciously. But has there ever been that hint of pity or paternalism in your thinking that I talked about in Chapter Three? It's sneaky, but it can easily exert an influence on anyone's thinking. I know, because I've been influenced by it myself.

The best remedy to these subtle prejudices is to meditate on how Jesus regarded the disabled. I've already touched on Jesus' attitude toward the disabled back in previous chapters. But let me emphasize just a few key points.

First, remember that Jesus' worldview was solidly based on the Old Testament. What do we find in the Old Testament about disabilities? Well, for starters, one of its biggest heroes, Moses, had a disability—a speech impairment (Ex. 4:10-12 and 6:12-30). Now, you might brush this off and think it was minor. Or, maybe you interpret this as mostly being in Moses' head—his excuse to avoid obeying God's call. But however severe it really was, God accommodated it, didn't He? He sent his brother Aaron to be Moses' spokesman (Ex. 4:14-17 and 7:1-3).

Or how about King David's treatment of Mephibosheth in 2 Samuel 9:1-13? Despite the way in which society in that era held disabled people in contempt, David showed that he was a man after God's heart by the way he helped this physically lame and land-deprived grandson of Saul. David gave him back his family land as well as an honored place at his own table.

God's regard for the disabled is even more explicit in the New Testament. Jesus' story of the "Great Banquet" (Luke 14:15-24) summarizes God's heart. In this story, God appears to desire the most marginalized in society to be present at His feast ("the poor, the crippled, the blind and the lame" vs. 21, NIV). God doesn't just include them. He actually seems eager to make them His guests ("compel them to come in," vs. 23, NIV). God wants to fill His house with the marginalized, including those marginalized by disability. Back in those days, it was common for the person hosting a party to send out two invitations.[30] The first was like a "save the date" invitation. The second was sent out, usually the day of the event, to tell guests the actual time. These two invitations had to happen because preparation of the meat was a lot less predictable in those days than it is now, and normally you didn't know ahead of time exactly when it would be ready.

In those days, people thought it was impolite to refuse the first invitation. Jesus' original audience would have recognized instantly how ridiculous the excuses were that people gave for declining that first invitation. They might even have found them humorous, until they realized that Jesus was making fun of their excuses for rejecting God's invitation. They all would have understood Jesus' meaning—that society's most marginalized were being taken into the Banquet ahead of them.

God still brings in the most marginalized, including the disabled, ahead of those who were first invited. The marginalized are still central in God's heart and value system. Jesus' treatment of the disabled confirms this. I don't need to rehearse for you the Bible's dozens and dozens of stories about this to remind you that this is a major theme in Jesus' ministry.

Before churches can do a good job of including the disabled, they need to be reminded of God's view of it all. So preach and teach about what God values and how God sees the disabled in order to help your congregation welcome them.

CULTIVATE AN ATTITUDE OF HOSPITALITY

The next most foundational way you can improve disability ministry is to cultivate an attitude of hospitality. Hospitality involves making guests feel welcome, even to the point of making them feel as though they belong in your house. True hospitality puts people at ease so that they can let down and be their true selves, as if they are family members.

A lot of churches are willing to do disability ministry, but they're not willing to welcome the disabled into their hearts as if they were family. Does your church make the disabled feel so welcome that they would feel as if they belong there? Is there an opportunity for them to feel as though they are family, or are they always just peripheral attendees?

COMMUNICATE ACCEPTANCE ABOVE ALL

Communicating acceptance to the disabled is one of the simplest but most powerful things you can do to improve disability ministry. It may sound like an oversimplification, but when you lead with acceptance you pave the way to be effective in all other aspects of ministry.

When I get into a stuck place with a person, I actually stop and pray and ask God to help me to make this person feel accepted. If the other person can feel accepted it will defuse anger, frustration, anxiety and other emotions that keep people feeling stuck. I've seen it work over and over again when I pray for that sense of acceptance. Even if there are communication barriers and we cannot understand one another completely, there is still a healthy respect that emerges from the attempt.

This culture of acceptance is what is needed most if you hope to include the disabled. It becomes a foundation for all other forms of ministry with the disabled. If the dominant message that disabled people feel from you and your church is, "I accept you no matter what," then it will generate a lot of good will and patience on their part. They will be able to overlook a lot of the mistakes and fumbles that you will inevitably make. If acceptance can become the atmosphere of your church then disabled people will be willing to put up with a lot of your church's shortcomings in disability ministry.

But if you don't communicate acceptance then all your other efforts are in vain. Disabled people can smell a lack of acceptance miles away. It won't matter how pretty and modern your wheelchair ramp is if the church doesn't exude acceptance.

One friend told me: "Church *was* a place I could go and talk to others with the same values. I work hard all week proving my abilities to others and I didn't expect to have to not only prove my ability, but my worth. I am made in God's image, but I feel like a thrown-out piece of trash." The lack of acceptance at church that this friend of mine experienced made her question her very sense of worth. She had previously looked to the church as a place free of worldly striving, where people didn't need to demonstrate their worth through what they could produce.

REDEFINE SUCCESS

Success is a loaded term with many meanings. Depending on how you define it, it can make or break your ministry with the disabled.

You see, a lot of people define success as accomplishing certain goals and finishing certain tasks. But for many disabled people, success cannot be so easily measured. There are some disabled people who cannot complete what others consider to be even a simple conversation. Such a person will not feel welcome in an environment in which success means completing tasks.

But if we can redefine success to mean any improvement in our mutual understanding of others, we're going to have a much better and more satisfying time with disability ministry. In the first chapter, I told a story of my attempt to talk with a friend who needed to point to letters in order to express himself. I told you how I botched that one with my impatience. We didn't finish a conversation in the same way that you and I might finish a conversation. But we did improve our mutual understanding, so I consider that time together to have been a success.

One of the things I learned from that experience was that sometimes I need help to make certain interactions work. The fact that I was willing to invest more time and energy into making it happen showed acceptance and respect, which he in turn felt. In general, the disabled are used to making adaptations. So even when you fumble around like I did that night, most will understand your desire is to better facilitate mutual understanding and not just to shut them down.

MAKE SUFFERING YOUR COMMON GROUND

A really powerful way to build bridges with the disabled is to emphasize our common experience with suffering. Suffering is about as universal an experience as there is, something to which everyone can relate. And God has wisdom for how Christians are to survive it, even thrive through it. By teaching and preaching about Christian suffering, you can help everyone in your congregation feel like we're all on the same level ground, as if we're all in this together.

There are numerous passages in both the Old and New Testaments about the place of suffering in the lives of believers. But let me highlight just one to make my point. Romans 5:1-5 talks about how suffering takes believers through a progression that eventually ends up in hope and love. Paul's phrase goes, "suffering produces perseverance; perseverance character, and character hope" (vs. 3-4, NIV). This is wonderful news for the disabled, who often feel like they are immersed in suffering every day.

You see, disabled people (and everyone for that matter) need to hear that suffering doesn't have to result in more misery. It can actually result in hope and being filled with God's love.

This can be a starting point for the disabled to find something in common with the church. The church has always suffered, and she continues to suffer up to this day. When you let non-disabled Christians get real and admit to their own struggles and suffering, you create an atmosphere in which disabled Christians can feel that they share in the same struggle. This can be powerfully healing for the disabled. And it can be powerfully inclusive.

INDIVIDUALIZE YOUR COMMUNICATION

Communication is one of the critical keys for disability ministry. As a church leader, I'm sure you've already figured out that your leadership success depends on finding creative ways to communicate uniquely with various individuals. You can send out that mass email addressed to everybody (and therefore nobody), but if you want your initiative to be successful, you know you need to give Sally a personal phone call, include some personal remarks in your email to Sam, and send a text to Frank. You probably already know that you need to over-communicate in order to actually be heard.

The same is true, and even more so, in disability ministry. John needs a personal, face-to-face visit to tell him about the upcoming meeting. Maria requires multiple reminders of the meeting, with a final reminder two hours before it begins. Jim needs someone with an accessible car to come and pick him up for the meeting. Sandra can only be present if she can Skype into the meeting. Every unique person requires individualized communication in a way that works for him or her.

"I don't have time for that!" You're saying right now. No one person does. So recruit more people into the disability ministry and let them experience its joys and challenges. Recruiting helpers will guarantee that more people in your congregation will gain a heart for disability ministry.

LIST ACCOMMODATIONS ON PRINTED MATERIALS AND THE WEBSITE

One very simple change you can make is to list out accommodations for the disabled in your printed materials and on your website. When a disabled person visits a church for the first time, or when he simply visits the church's website, he needs to know right away what the accommodations are. This helps him make a quick evaluation of whether or not to pursue involvement in this church.

But if this information is hard to access, or if someone has to look in several locations before finding all the pertinent details, then a disabled person may feel discouraged from seeking it out. If a blind visitor comes to you, the church leader, to ask about materials printed in Braille, and you have to redirect her to another person who must then redirect her again to yet a third person, then your church probably isn't worth the effort to join.

Or if a website visitor must navigate through several obscure pages before finding out any information about accommodations then he will be hesitant to come there in person. Why should he make a huge effort to visit in person when it is hard to quickly find out online how you're going to smooth out the barriers that he faces?

But if the accommodations are easy and quick to access, then the would-be disabled visitor can know right away that you already have a culture of acceptance. Such a list immediately communicates that you care enough that he can confidently expect to find a welcome within your walls.

One last point about communicating your accommodating materials on your church's website. If you list your ministries make sure you list disability ministry as well. When a potential visitor who is disabled sees this listed, it will assure her that your church is likely a safe place. Then, when you explain the importance of this ministry keep your definition short but powerful. Here's an example you can use: "Our disability ministry encourages a culture of acceptance of all God's children including those affected by disabilities." Just a single sentence but it communicate volumes to the disabled.

In this current world of so much hate and bitterness, this idea of creating a culture of acceptance will not only help the disabled. It will also encourage others in your to grow in the acceptance of differences. That's a win-win for everyone in your church.

JUST ASK ME

One of the most important strategies for welcoming the disabled into your church is to simply ask what their needs are.

Don't assume you know what they need, like "all quadriplegics require this and that for successful ministry." Take the time and show enough respect to simply ask.

I was visiting a church recently and there was a huge discussion of wheelchairs during worship. They were having five to six chairs a service and the board was concerned they were a fire hazard that would block the aisle. So they asked that anyone using a chair or a walker sit in the back. But this was painful to those using the mobility aids, since some wanted to be nearer to the front where all the action was. This new policy made them feel alienated. Someone asked me what I thought would work. I suggested a few ideas, such as removing the very first row of pews or perhaps a set of three pews on the side where nobody sat. I told them that I really had no idea what would work best. So I asked what the chair users thought about it. I was met with a silence from the board members that was so heavy. I cleared my throat and asked if I had said something wrong. One of the board members spoke up and sheepishly admitted that he never thought to ask. I smiled and told them that this may not even be an issue, but they would never know if they didn't ask.

This church eventually did find a solution collectively and now their leadership meets with disabled people once a quarter in order to brainstorm how to better welcome people with disabilities.

Think about having houseguests from another country. Most likely upon first welcoming them you would ask something like, "what would help make your stay enjoyable?" This does several important things right away. First, it opens the door for them to voice their needs. It communicates to them that all of their needs are acceptable and reasonable in your mind. A lot of disabled people worry about rejection because others perceive their needs as too "high maintenance." But by simply asking about their needs, you show that their needs are not a deal breaker. It shows that fulfilling their needs is important to you. This attitude alone will make all your interactions start off on the right foot. The disabled person will understand you are showing respect and not pity.

But people often hesitate to ask about the needs of the disabled. This hesitation is understandable. It usually arises from various fears. For instance, you may hesitate to ask, "How can I help?" because you're worried about the reaction of the disabled individual. You think, "Perhaps this person is touchy about his disability. I better not mention it." But think about it this way: yes, it is possible that you will hurt someone's feelings by mentioning a painful subject. But it is a lot more possible that you will hurt his feelings if you pretend his disability is invisible and say nothing at all. Why? Because first of all, if you don't ask, you're in much greater danger of making a mistake that really could hurt that person. For example, if you don't find out the best way to move someone's wheelchair, you risk serious injury. But worse yet, if you treat a person's disability as invisible, you're really treating his whole being as invisible. Do you like to be treated as if you're invisible?

You might hesitate to ask because you imagine that simply asking will offend a disabled person. Some non-disabled people think to themselves, "She must be so ashamed of her disability. If I ask her about it, it will be like I'm pointing out the thing that shames her. My questions will draw attention to it but I'm sure she'd prefer to divert attention from it." This is an understandable worry, because most people don't like their shortcomings and flaws pointed out, even when they're obvious. But you need to understand something: the great majority of disabled people have already come to accept their disability as part of normal life. The great majority has already accepted themselves as disabled people. Most of us have gotten over any shame associated with it.

But when you don't ask us, you actually increase the shame. Your silence makes it seem like there is something to be ashamed of. I know I've got an obvious disability. I know that you know it. Why pretend that it isn't there? It actually reduces the shame to make a simple inquiry about it. Asking brings everything out into the light and doesn't allow shame to fester.

You might hesitate to ask because it is difficult for you to articulate questions in the first place. Again, this is understandable. Sometimes you may never have been exposed to a certain kind of disability before, and you can't even imagine what the person's adaptations and needs may be. So of course you don't know where to begin asking. But here's the thing: people with disabilities, and especially people with rare disabilities, already know that they need to educate others if they expect help from them. They already realize that people might be surprised, caught off guard, and perplexed by the disability. They aren't surprised at your confusion and lack of exposure. Most people with disabilities would rather you ask any question, even if at first it is the wrong question, than have you be silent and risk endangering them with your ignorance. In cases when you're not sure even where to begin, the best thing to do is simply say politely, "Sorry, I've not encountered this before. Could you help me understand this a little better?" The disabled person already knows what you need to know.

Some people hesitate to ask because they want to appear as if they already know it all. We all invest a lot in appearing to be competent. All of us closely manages our public image. But in the case of helping the disabled, you're not doing anyone any favors, least of all your image, by pretending that you already know everything. If you avoid asking because you want to keep up your image, you run the risk of truly endangering someone. As I've already said, every disabled person has unique modifications and adaptations. There are as many iterations of a certain kind of disability as there are people with that disability. It is always most respectful to assume that, however much experience you've already had with a certain disability, this person's expression of it is unique. It is always best to find out the unique ways you can handle *this* particular case.

When non-disabled people hesitate to ask, disabled people may interpret it as rejection. In reality, this is more a communication barrier than actual rejection, but you can understand why it feels like rejection. How does it feel to you when others ignore something very significant in your life? When others refuse to acknowledge an important part of you, doesn't it feel like they don't want all of you? This is how it feels to disabled people when people fail to ask them about their needs. Most disabled people just wish that someone would ask for their opinion about a physical or relational barrier. And when you ask, remember to listen to the answer carefully. Don't fall into the trap of so many church leaders who imagine that a disabled person doesn't understand her own challenges as well as you do.

When you do ask about accommodations, I should warn you to proceed with caution. The person you are asking needs to understand that you have good intentions for asking these questions. So, I would recommend that you practice this conversation ahead of time. It might sound silly, but it will actually make it feel less awkward when it is time to discuss accommodations. Practicing will help you sound more natural. That way, when you do have the discussion about accommodations, you're conversation will match your leadership style and personal gifts.

I have a funny example from my life of how I mistook the intentions of someone who didn't ask before trying to help. It shows how even great intentions can be misinterpreted. One busy evening my hubby and I were preparing to sit down to supper with some friends. It was a loud and chaotic environment. My hubby, who knows my likes, put a plate together for me. Well, I was struggling with some self-esteem issues at the time, and so I took this gesture as a sign that he did not think I was capable of choosing what I wanted. Worse yet, I took it as a sign that my thinking and desires didn't matter.

My hubby was genuinely concerned and defensive when I confronted him later about it. His intent was to be sweet. Unfortunately, my circumstances were such that I took it as controlling. Was my hubby to blame? No, of course not. Was I wrong? Probably. But something or someone has hurt me enough in this area that others' efforts to help can tend to rekindle these feelings. In other words, it was a sore spot for me because I'd been hurt by others before who "helped" when they assumed I was incapable.

Due to great communication my husband and I worked it out. Now we can chuckle over the infamous incident of fixing a taco salad. My husband chose to show me compassion even if I was being unreasonable. He chose to value me and ultimately that is what we need to do for others. So, the moral of the story is to show compassion and show that you value others by asking first.

PROMOTE NETWORKING AMONG DISABLED PEERS

As my experiment with Sawubona made clear, it is essential that disabled believers network with each other. Most of the disabled people who might want to attend your church know other disabled people through various social services. But not all the would-be disabled attenders are connected with other disabled *believers*. So, you have a great opportunity to cultivate intimate, biblical community among the disabled if you can help them get connected to their peers.

This kind of community doesn't necessarily have to be as high a level of commitment as Sawubona was. The commit level of intentional communities exists along a wide spectrum, some requiring more commitment than others. But any amount of networking that you can encourage among the disabled creates powerfully fruitful support systems.

For example, one way that Sawubona increased participation in church activities was that it helped us share our resources with each other. Since all our members were legally blind, we all shared the need for more resources that help the blind. Because of our networking, those of us with stronger resources for the blind were able to connect our fellow members to those resources. We could give each other tutorials and advice for how to use the resources better. We shared with each other how to access Scriptures, commentaries and other resources to improve our ability to interact in Bible studies or other church-related activities. If we hadn't supported each other this way, several of our members would never have had the confidence to jump into church participation like we did.

Also, do you remember how I said earlier that for each of us Sawubona increased a sense of being accepted? That sense of acceptance didn't come because our local churches were necessarily doing anything differently. It came because we had helped one another with self-acceptance, and because we worked to build up each other's confidence. That's what networking can do better than what you can do alone.

The networking also helped us overcome the sense of inadequacy that we all felt when we interacted with churches. Whenever one of us tried a new experience or made a new effort to participate in our local church, that person would come back to Sawubona and relate the experience, including what worked and what didn't. This process helped us all figure out why certain activities were harder or less successful than others. If something wasn't successful, the group was able to determine which resources and skills were probably missing. Once we figured that out, we were able to go back to our local churches with more wisdom and determination to succeed. This wouldn't have happened if a non-disabled person had simply said, "I know what went wrong. This is the answer..."

FIND VOLUNTEER OPPORTUNITIES THAT MAKE US FEEL LIKE ASSETS

Many disabled people feel more like burdens than assets. There are all kinds of things in our day-to-day lives that reinforce this impression. For example, a lot of disabled people may rely on government assistance for living expenses. This can make us feel like a burden on society instead of a contributor. But despite this feeling, disabled people also know that they have valuable resources to help others. So, churches can be inclusive by finding ways that disabled people can share their gifts and strengths and resources.

For example, a disabled person might love helping with computer issues. Another may perhaps have a talent for reading aloud. I know of a church in which many of its senior members had to go into a nursing home. A new member attending the church loved to visit these older members and read the Bible to them. Together they all built relationships and strengthened each other's faith. This new member, who happened to be paralyzed, learned so much from these elders. Moreover, the elders were blessed by the visits.

Do you see what I'm talking about? This paralyzed person was made to feel like an asset instead of a burden because she knew she had something significant that she could contribute. Her paralysis didn't hinder her from blessing the senior members in a way that was very important to them.

There are so many creative opportunities you can give your disabled members—always be on the hunt for them.

INVOLVE THE DISABLED IN LEADERSHIP

An important strategy for success is to involve the disabled in leadership. This includes everything from intentionally helping a disabled person get elected to the church board, to having an easy way for the disabled to give feedback directly to the leadership. Because the disabled are so often the most neglected among us, church leaders are frequently unaware of their needs or concerns. This is especially true when there is no voice from a disabled person on a governing board.

It is hard for some disabled people to pick up a phone and call the pastor directly. It is hard for others to send the pastor an email. It is even harder for some to visit the church physically during the week to connect with the pastor one-on-one. So, leadership needs to figure out creative ways to make sure the voice of the disabled is heard loudly and regularly.

I have encouraged churches to call on a group of church members who can serve as ambassadors for the disabled. I suggest that church leadership should meet with such a group at least quarterly in order to ask for help or to hear feedback about how programs are working. You'll be amazed at how eager some people are to give constructive feedback. I recommend pulling together a group with various disabilities represented so that you get a sense of what is and isn't working for people. For instance, a blind person is going to give you completely different feedback than a quadriplegic. You need to hear both.

You might be thinking, "but we only have one or two people (or none!) with disabilities here. Who is supposed to serve as an ambassador?" If you're in that situation, simply ask people who are seniors to serve. Most senior citizens have experienced a debilitating condition, or they are afraid of one right around the corner. Use their wisdom because they will be able to tell you exactly what it is like to find your bathroom inaccessible, your bulletin print too small to read and your leadership dismissive of their gifts.

One practice that we do as a ministry is to actively include on our board of directors people with a testimony of disability. The members either have a disability themselves, or they have a family member who is affected by a disability. This has kept our ministry fresh and it has kept us geared up for ministry with the disabled. With such people in the top circle of leadership at Seek the Son, we've been able to prevent blind spots like the one I experienced when I sought to serve as a camp counselor or like when I was pursuing my pastoral ordination.

You might not have a large enough pool of disabled people at your church to include someone on the board. But if you do, it will go a long way to have this voice at your top level of leadership.

When leadership is closely connected with people who are disabled, a lot of progress can be made. People who study diversity have found that in order for an organization to become friendlier to people of diverse backgrounds, the leadership must become "champions" of that diversity. That's what Howard Ross says, who has been studying how to make organizations more diverse for over 25 years.[31] In his book *Reinventing Diversity*, he says that in order for diversity initiatives to be successful, the leadership has to adopt as their own the idea that diversity is a good thing and that the organization would be better off if it were more diverse.[32]

The same is true when it comes to ministering with disabled people. If you want disabled people to feel welcome, leadership must become their champion. Leadership must come to see their inclusion and empowerment as something that is good for the whole church and for the Kingdom of God.

But the leadership can't just give lip service to the idea of including people with disabilities. Taylor Cox Jr., another researcher of diversity, writes that leaders must champion the cause both verbally and in personal practice.[33] He writes that "leadership cannot be delegated,"[34] but that leaders must live out the value of diversity if it is going to be successful. Cox draws on examples from several companies that successfully made their organizations more diverse, like Xerox, Corning, and Avon. These companies succeeded in these efforts because they had leaders who were committed to the vision of diversity.[35]

The same is true of including the disabled. Unless your leadership is committed to the vision of enabling the disabled, in both word and deed, you won't be successful at it. This can begin by making sure that leadership is closely connected with the disabled.

INCORPORATE THE DISABLED IN WORSHIP

Almost as important as involving the disabled in church leadership is to involve the disabled in the worship ministry. Disabled people suffer for being invisible in most communities. Under this cloak of invisibility, negative stereotypes, fears and discomfort fester and grow. But participation in Sunday morning worship makes the disabled visible, which in turn banishes those stereotypes and anxieties.

When disabled people can serve in the public worship ministry, it communicates several things. First, it shows the congregation that at this church, we embrace the disabled. We embrace them enough to include them in this all-important ministry. Second, it says, "there are no barriers to participate at this church." It reminds the congregation every single week that there is no obstacle to every single person participating fully in the ministry. Finally, it communicates that we are a community of love rather than a community that expects people to measure up before they can get involved.

These are messages that the disabled need to hear from your church. These are some of the strategies that will help the disabled feel that they can fully participate in your congregation. But best of all, if the disabled are hearing this message, you can know that everybody is hearing this message. And don't you want everybody to hear this message?

Chapter Six

Teach Second-Class Citizens of the World the Privileges and Responsibilities of Being First-Class Citizens of Heaven

Once you've begun to work on the basic things described in the previous two chapters, you're ready to do one of the most powerful parts of disability ministry: teach the privileges and responsibilities of being a first-class citizen of heaven.

Remember, most of us come to church feeling like second-class citizens of this world. It is like baggage that we carry in with us. We all feel defective in one way or another. Some of this comes from experiences of rejection that every disabled person has experienced. Maybe the rejection first happened on the playground as a child, when other children refused to play because we couldn't do certain things. Whenever it first came, the message has only been reinforced in the rest of our adult lives. Simply put, much of life feels inaccessible. Whenever or however it began, most of us come in to church feeling beat up by the world. Most of us have absorbed the message that we are inferior, unable to contribute to society like others do, and therefore "second-class."

This sense of being a second-class citizen often gets reinforced and perpetuated at church. Some churches promote the idea that to be involved, you need to have a certain level of energy and capacity. This can leave us with feelings of inadequacy. Lots of disabled people report that church communities tend to remind them of what they cannot do, rather than what they can. It makes us feel like we're burdens rather than assets.

Part of your job is to help us realize that no matter what the world makes us feel like, we are actually first-class citizens of heaven. One of the key elements of being a first-class citizen instead of a second-class citizen is that you have both privileges and responsibilities. For instance, first-class American citizens have both the privilege to vote for our leaders and the corresponding responsibility to participate in local self-government. First-class American citizens have privileges to drive on public highways and educate their children at public schools, as well as the corresponding responsibility to pay taxes so those things get funded. The two always go hand-in-hand for first-class citizens. The same is true for first-class citizens of heaven.

It is important for disabled believers to learn or be reminded of both their privileges and responsibilities as citizens of heaven and as members of your church. Of course, it goes without saying that it is encouraging and empowering simply to know our privileges. But knowing that we have responsibilities is also encouraging and empowering in its own way. A person with responsibilities feels ownership for his community, and therefore feels that he has a stake in its welfare. A person with responsibilities feels more motivated to do something to improve his community.

You want all your members to know both their privileges and

responsibilities, but it is especially important for your disabled members to know them. For the disabled, this is one of the most attractive things about being a part of a local church. In a world that shouts at us, "you are second-class citizens" at every turn, churches can stand out in sharp contrast to the world and give us instead this message: "you are *first*-class citizens of heaven." No other institution or tradition or organization can really give us that message—just the church.

I told you earlier that if you will genuinely welcome and empower the disabled believers into your church, you will unleash a powerful force of loyal disciples who are deeply devoted to Jesus and who are highly fruitful in His service, for the good of your whole church and its surrounding community. This empowerment will come if they know their privileges and responsibilities, since it will make them feel the pride and sense of ownership that only first-class citizens feel in a society.

Privileges and responsibilities always go hand in hand. You can't separate one from the other. So, as you'll see, all the privileges I am about to describe are also responsibilities and visa-versa.

DISCOVER AND APPLY YOUR NEW IDENTITY IN CHRIST

Back in Chapter Three I talked about the need to discover and apply our new identity in Christ. This is a responsibility as well as a privilege. As a minister of the Gospel, one of your chief duties is to teach this idea to the disabled at your church. One's new identity in Christ is the foundation for understanding all of our other responsibilities and privileges. So, it is critical that disabled people learn this new identity and be encouraged to apply it.

If an American citizen did not know her identity as an

American, she would lose all motivation to participate in the community for the public good. Why would she participate if she did not feel as if she were a stakeholder? For instance, let's say someone immigrates to the US from another country. There is often a long period of several years before she earns her citizenship and can exercise her rights, privileges and responsibilities. In that waiting time, she won't do any of the things that fully naturalized, first-class citizens do because she has no reason to do them. She won't contact her representatives to fight for necessary improvements in the community. She won't voice her opinions about local political issues because she is probably just trying to fit in and doesn't want to make any enemies. She'll be careful not to draw overly on any entitlements because she realizes that she doesn't yet really have a right to them. She knows that access to them might be removed in an instant. She might not feel the need to clean up the area around her property because she feels no sense of obligation to anything beyond what she directly owns. She might not feel concern for the welfare, safety and prosperity of her neighbors because she doesn't see her welfare, safety and prosperity inextricably tied up with theirs. She certainly won't vote because she can't legally do it.

But once she has become a citizen and has absorbed her new identity, then you almost can't stop her from making robust contributions to the public good. She sees herself as a stakeholder now, simply because she now sees her identity as an American instead of as a "foreigner." A new sense of confidence swells her spirit and enables her to soar to new heights.

One of the members of Sawubona told the rest of us that in her church she was known simply as "the blind woman with a yellow dog." She realized in the course of Sawubona that many people at church did not even know her first name. Being known this way, instead of by her new identity in Christ, demotivated her from fully participating. She realized that she needed to start acting as if her new identity in Christ really mattered. So, she began by casually interjecting her name so that people could find out that she had an identity other than "that blind woman." Then, she started to call herself "daughter of the King" or "child of God." This shift in thinking, and the shift in how she communicated about herself, started to improve this woman's involvement at church. First, it empowered her to be more bold and friendly. Second, it sparked people to be more attentive toward her in return. People discovered her confidence in her new identity and were attracted to it. When she told the Sawubona group about this, we all copied her and began to experience a similar growth in confidence and ownership.

This woman's confidence came from her knowledge of her new identity in Christ. Knowing her privileged status as a "daughter of the king" led her to have more confidence and strengthened her ability to participate in church life.

So, take some time to review Theme #1 back in Chapter Four. Do some Bible study about our new identity in Christ and prepare a teaching about this topic. Tell the disabled among you about their status as beloved children of God (John 1:12, 1 John 3:1). Teach them about their nature as objects of grace and mercy (Eph. 1; Rom. 5:8, 9:22-23). Show them their dignity as victors over all darkness (Rom. 8:27-38, Eph. 6:10-20, 2 Cor. 2:14). Highlight to your disabled audience how Christians will be entrusted with ruling the new heaven and the new earth alongside Jesus Himself (1 Cor. 6:2-3, 2 Tim. 2:12, Rev. 20:4-6).

But don't just stop at the privileges. Show them how these privileges translate into responsibilities. For instance, when Paul reminded the Corinthians about their future status of ruling with Christ, he had an agenda for telling them this. He wanted them to change their behavior now, in this life, in light of their future status. He didn't just want them to feel good about themselves and about their future. He wrote it to improve their behavior and heal their rifts here and now. Study the context of Chapter 6 in 1 Corinthians and you'll see what I mean. Their future glorious status was meant to inflame their sense of responsibility about how to act in this life.

Just like with the Sawubona member I described above, it will enflame the disabled in your congregation with a sense of duty toward the rest of the community when they know these truths about a Christian's identity in Christ.

PRAYER

Prayer is one of the greatest privileges and responsibilities of a first-class citizen of heaven. If the disabled among you get ahold of this message, you'll be a part of raising up a new army of spiritual warriors who are ready to dive into the deep end of church involvement.

The privilege of prayer comes directly out of our new identity in Christ. Because we have been given the right to become children of God (John 1:12, 1 John 3:1), we now have the honor to appear in His presence without any mediators and to be heard directly by His compassionate ear (Ps. 40:1, Heb. 4:16, 10:19). This God sits on a "throne of grace" (Heb. 4:16, NIV) and wields total authority over all things in the heavens and on the earth (Matt. 28:18, Phil. 2:9-11, Col. 1:15-21). Thus, He is able to answer your boldest, brashest prayer.

But prayer isn't amazing only because the One on the throne is all-powerful. It is amazing because this omnipotent God can, "empathize with our weaknesses" (Heb. 4:15, NIV). He listens to us with a tender ear that recognizes how frail and little we are.

Best of all, God is generous and He wants to answer our prayers (Luke 11:5-8, James 1:5).

What's more, Jesus enables us to stand before God the Father, "holy in his sight, without blemish and free from accusation" (Col. 1:22, NIV). So, those of us in Christ have nothing to hinder our being heard by God. Because of this, we are exhorted to "approach" this empathetic and all-powerful ear, "so that we may receive mercy and find grace to help us in the time of need" (Heb. 4:16, NIV). This same verse says we may draw near "with confidence." Later in Hebrews, the author says that this confidence comes, "by the blood of Jesus" (10:19, NIV) and by virtue of His successful intercession as High Priest on our behalf (10:21, NIV). This gives us confidence, allowing us to come to Him, "with the full assurance of faith" (10:22, NIV), because His blood and priestly work have cleansed us from all wickedness that offends God and that could block our prayer.

This confidence and assurance also empower us to ask God "whatever ... for anything" (John 14:13-14, NIV). This means that God is willing to entertain unlimited possibilities of requests from us. We can know when we ask for this "whatever" in Jesus' name that He "will do it" (vs. 14, NIV). This promise of answered prayer is so expansive that it is bound to be good news to the disabled person who has mostly received a dismissive "no" to most of his requests for help out in the world.

Think of how life changing it would be for a disabled person, disempowered by life and made to feel like a second-class citizen everywhere else, to get ahold of this truth. Talk about access! No wheelchair ramps needed! Just simple faith in your heart through Jesus, and you get to speak directly with God, with full assurance of being heard, cared for, and answered by the Sovereign Lord of the universe. Talk about empowerment!

So the good news about prayer can be especially heartening

to the disabled. Back in Chapter 2, I talked about how Paul the Apostle struggled with a disability. We don't know what exactly the disability was, but in 2 Corinthians 12 Paul describes how God used it for the success of his ministry rather than for his failure. One reason for this was that disability showed Paul how to cry out in prayer. This crying out (2 Cor. 12:7-10) was not merely a bitter rant against his lot in life. It was a way of dialoguing with the Lord about these challenges. It was his way of inviting God into the suffering. It was his way to obtain grace during his suffering. Paul handled his pain by praying to the Lord.

So, this passage directs disabled believers to the powerful resource of prayer. It is by prayer that the disabled can access the direct help of the Lord and receive His comfort in the midst of the trials associated with disabilities.

But prayer isn't only a privilege. It is also an important responsibility. For instance, Paul clearly felt it was his duty to pray for those churches he'd planted, judging from the extra time he took to describe his prayers for them (Eph. 1:15-19, 3:14-19, Col. 1:9-14). Paul also exhorted his readers to pray for him (Eph. 6:19-20, Col. 4:3-4) with a kind of desperation that makes you feel as if he depended on these prayers. Paul actually commanded the Colossians, "*devote* yourselves to prayer, being watchful and thankful" (Col. 4:2, NIV). He commanded the Ephesians, "be alert and always keep on praying for all the saints" (6:18, NIV). He commanded the Thessalonians to "pray continually" (1 Thess. 5:17, NIV).

The Apostle Peter had a similar view of the necessity of prayer. In his first letter, he wrote to husbands, "be considerate as you live with your wives, and treat them with respect as the weaker partner and as heirs with you of the gracious gift of life, so that nothing will hinder your prayers" (1 Pet. 3:7, NIV). Prayer is so important that in order to faithfully practice it we need to treat one another well. Later he writes, "be alert and of sober mind so that you may pray" (4:7, NIV). Prayer is so necessary that Peter commands us to cultivate clear mindedness and self-control so that we can do it well.

Jesus never told His disciples *"If* you pray," as if prayer were optional. He said, *"when* you pray," (Matt. 6:5, NIV), with the clear assumption that they would pray and that it was a normal part of the life of a disciple. Jesus told one of His most famous parables, "to show them that they should always pray and not give up" (Luke 18:1-8, NIV). Jesus intended His followers to pray and to pray with perseverance.

When disabled believers learn of the privileges and responsibilities of prayer, it is like setting off a bomb in the church. Suddenly, disempowered believers are empowered and encouraged. When they realize the authority and the capacity for successful ministry that comes with prayer, you won't be able to hold back the disabled from being your most faithful and productive members.

FORGIVE

Forgiveness is a responsibility of every person who has ever bowed a knee to Jesus' lordship and sworn, "I will follow You." No matter how awful the discrimination you've faced, no matter how severe, you are responsible to God to forgive. Forgiveness is also one of Christianity's most delightful privileges. When we forgive we are released from the chains of bitterness and resentment, two of the heaviest burdens anyone can ever bear. Disabled people are called to forgive as much as any other follower of Jesus.

Jesus expected His followers to forgive those who had harmed them. He wove this expectation into the prayer that He gave us all to pray (Matt. 6:12, 14-15, Luke 11:4). He taught His disciples that forgiveness was necessary, and that if we didn't forgive, our prayers would be hindered (Mark 11:25). He ordered us to forgive our brothers when they repent (Luke 17:3). He explained to His disciples that they were to forgive without limit (Matt. 18:15-20). When Jesus died on the cross, He modeled forgiveness (Luke 23:34) and expected us to follow this example.

Paul also taught that we ought to forgive (2 Cor. 2:7). He tells us to imitate Jesus' forgiveness when he writes, "Bear with each other and forgive one another if any of you has a grievance against someone. Forgive as the Lord forgave you" (Col. 3:13, NIV). He wrote almost the same thing to the Ephesians: "Be kind and compassionate to one another, forgiving each other, just as in Christ God forgave you" (Eph. 4:32, NIV). Paul's logic is pretty obvious here: since we, who opposed God, received this undeserved forgiveness from Him, we ought to extend undeserved forgiveness to those who have opposed us.

It is clear: the Bible teaches that we are required to forgive. But a lot of disabled people struggle to forgive because most of us have experienced so many hurts in life. We often feel as if we've received worse treatment than the average person. That may or may not always be true, but if you feel that way, it is hard to overcome the perception. Besides, it can be hard to forgive when people keep committing the same offenses against you. For instance, almost every disabled person can give you a long list of times he has experienced discrimination because of his disability. It gets so tiring to deal with the same issue over and over again.

What's more, it is harder to forgive when you're the more vulnerable person in a relationship. What I mean is, if you're the more vulnerable one, then forgiveness can feel like you're willingly signing up again to be hurt and taken advantage of. It can feel like you're broadcasting, "hey, I'm naked and exposed with nothing to protect me. Come and get me!" And for people who already feel so naked and exposed, it can feel downright foolish to forgive.

Think about it. Un-forgiveness can feel like a protective barrier that keeps out those who would hurt you. When you forgive, it can feel like you are naively letting down the wall of protection. Would you willingly place yourself in a vulnerable position where people can do you more harm? Many disabled people already feel like we're exposed to more harm than the average person. Why should we willingly sign up for more?

I recently heard of a church in which several leaders were found to be guilty of molesting children entrusted to their care. In a misguided application of Jesus' teaching on forgiveness, these children were made to face their offenders and tell them "I forgive you." This was wrong for so many reasons. First of all, it was wrong because the children were compelled to say "I forgive you." If you haven't figured it out yet, no one can be compelled to forgive from the heart. But what was especially wrong about this story was that the vulnerable ones, the children, were put back under the power of the powerful ones, the perpetrators, when they were made to meet face-to-face. When they had to say, "I forgive you," they were made to take down their little protective barriers and say to their perpetrators, "I'm vulnerable to you all over again. I'm unprotected and exposed again." This basically re-traumatizes vulnerable people and doesn't allow them to heal.

For the disabled, it can feel the same way when churches tell us, "you must forgive" without addressing the cause of the hurt, or without addressing the benefits of forgiveness. Why would we put ourselves in such a position, just to get re-traumatized?

So your job as a minister of the Gospel is to help your disabled parishioners understand how Jesus both requires forgiveness and how He protects us and empowers us so that we can forgive. You need to explain the benefits of forgiveness and how those benefits outweigh the costs. You need to do this while being sensitive to our vulnerability. The best way to do this is to help us address the cause of the hurts. For instance, if a disabled congregant is offended because your church's bathrooms are inaccessible, help address the problem. Yes, this person needs to forgive. But she also has a real need and your job is to help find a solution. If you don't help solve the problem, you're just setting up this person to get offended again and again. And you're setting him up to make forgiveness nearly impossible because his heart will just get harder and harder as each week passes and the problem goes unsolved.

I want to share a little of my journey with forgiveness and what God brought out of it. Do you remember my story back in Chapter Three about my ordination? Do you remember how that disability ministry had denied me the honor of working at a summer camp because they assumed I was unable to carry out the duties? Do you remember how they refused to celebrate my ordination because of my gender? Back then, my confusion and hurt were complicated because, since we worked as missionaries, I needed to explain to our supporters about my decision not to continue with this organization. How was I going to deal with all this?

I easily could have ranted and created quite a scene. But one thing became clear in that situation—the people I would have upset with my ranting already knew this bitter grief. They were the ones who had kept telling me about it over and over again. I didn't need to provide them with any more evidence of the church's serious problem with discrimination. They already knew about it. So, part of my decision to forgive came from the realization that I didn't want to create even more hurt.

As I sought God about what to do, He showed me two important things. First, He showed me His love. He loved the people in the disability ministry with whom I had worked, and He loved the people they were trying to help. He was calling me to love as well. He wanted me to bring healing and not more fury. He wanted me to stand up for rights but not bring down other people who were trying to help. This was how I discovered the motivation to forgive them.

The second thing God showed me was His great power. By His own power, He had allowed this rift to occur because He was using it to open my eyes. It has opened my eyes to the reality of what it is like to feel as if you are an outsider in a church family. Prior to this ordeal, my experience with church had been so positive. But this experience showed me it isn't positive for everyone with disabilities. The pain of this realization awoke deep compassion in me for disabled brothers and sisters in Christ. Now I knew how so many of them feel every day.

This awakening of compassion led to an even more startling revelation: God told me that He wanted Ken and me to start our own disability ministry, one that would work specifically toward the cause of reconciliation. So that is what we did. That is how Seek the Son Ministries began.

So just as I accepted my call to serve God as an ordained pastor, God revealed to me how exactly I was to serve: through the creation of my own disability ministry. And He revealed this through the agony of the other ministry's rejection. If Paul could talk about his ministry as a form of labor akin to painful childbirth ("My dear children, for whom I am again in the pains of childbirth until Christ is formed in you," Gal. 4:19, NIV), then why wouldn't God give birth to a new ministry through my painful ordeal?

But I wouldn't have discovered any of this if I had chosen to hold on to my bitterness against the other disability ministry. It was by choosing acceptance and by practicing forgiveness that I was able to walk through the open doorway and start the new ministry. I experienced forgiveness as both a privilege and as a responsibility.

It is the same for you. If you hold on to your bitterness, you will only poison yourself and limit your own ability to be used by God. But if you will choose forgiveness, you will open yourself up to God's amazing possibilities.

WORK TOWARD RECONCILIATION

Forgiveness is just one step in the larger process of reconciliation. Sawubona existed to help work toward reconciliation between churches and the disabled. The ministry I lead, Seek the Son, is all about reconciliation. I want to see churches and disabled people reconciled to one another. I want to see them enjoying all the benefits of being in relationship with each other. It is God's ultimate goal for all relationships.

Jesus thought that reconciliation was so important that He told His disciples to leave their gifts in front of the alter and go to be reconciled with other people. They were to offer their gifts only after that was done (Matt. 5:24). He told them "try hard to be reconciled" with their adversaries, before they get into trouble over being divided (Luke 12:58, NIV).

Paul made clear that reconciliation between people was one of the reasons why Jesus died on the cross:

> For he himself is our peace, who has made the two groups one and has destroyed the barrier, the dividing wall of hostility, by setting aside in his flesh the law with its commands and regulations. His purpose was

to create in himself one new humanity out of the two,
thus making peace, and in one body to reconcile both
of them to God through the cross, by which he put to
death their hostility. Eph. 2:15-16, NIV

For Paul, reconciliation is the inevitable outcome of applying the cross to our relationships. In his letter to the Philippians, he takes space from the main thrust of his argument to urge two women, Syntyche and Euodia, to be reconciled (Phil. 4:2-3). Of all the things that Paul could have written about in that space, he took the time to urge reconciliation between just two people in the church.

Like forgiveness, reconciliation is both a Christian responsibility and a privilege. And like forgiveness, it is both required and it offers glorious benefits to those who go through its full process. As with forgiveness, it is your job to teach your congregants about reconciliation. In Syntyche and Euodia's situation, Paul specifically asked church leadership to assist with the reconciliation process (Phil. 4:3).

Reconciliation has many steps, and one of the best ways you can minister to disabled people is to lay out the steps and show them how to proceed through them. The full process of reconciliation can be daunting because it can feel overwhelmingly complicated. It can appear as if there are too many steps. It can be hard to endure all the steps to achieve true reconciliation. It often feels much easier just to cut people off and ignore them.

One of the things we discovered in Sawubona was that we all needed a lot of coaching and support in order to reconcile with others. Each of us would come to the group and say, "I'm struggling with this or that person" or "I'm struggling with church leadership." The rest of us would pray for them, encourage them and give them advice about the steps to take toward reconciliation. This is the kind of support you can offer to disabled people who are seeking to reconcile. In addition to teaching the steps of reconciliation, you can be like a coach in this process. Your prayers, support and situation-specific advice can go a long way to help people progress through the process of reconciliation.

IDENTIFY AND USE YOUR SPIRITUAL GIFTS

One of the most powerful things you can do for your disabled congregants is to help them identify and use their spiritual gifts. Paul wrote to the Corinthians "When you come together, *each of you* has a hymn, or a word of instruction, a revelation, a tongue or an interpretation" (1 Cor. 14:26a, NIV). *Each* church member brings some sort of contribution. *Each* contribution helps the larger group, "so that the church may be built up." (26:b, NIV).

You've already read back in Chapter Four how a discussion of spiritual gifts consumed a large part of our first few weeks of Sawubona. I put everyone through a spiritual gifts assessment and then I did a lot of teaching about it. This sparked long conversions among us. Ultimately, it was one of the main things that launched the Sawubona members into more fruitful church participation.

You need to start by teaching the disabled that they do have spiritual gifts. As I've already written, many of us have been led to believe that we don't even have spiritual gifts in the first place. You need to correct that error with your teaching so that every person, of whatever level of disability, knows she or he has spiritual gifts from God. This alone is an incredibly powerful way to motivate and encourage the disabled.

Second, you need to teach that their spiritual gifts matter. Many believe that even if they have spiritual gifts they don't matter and we can't make a difference with them. But Paul wrote, "those parts of the body that seem to be weaker are indispensible" (1 Cor. 12:22). You need to drum into the hearts and minds of your disabled congregants that their gifts, and therefore their presence at church, are *indispensible* to the functioning of the whole body. Your church can't do without them. Your church can't do what it is called to do, or reach whom it is called to reach, or help those it is called to help, without *everyone's* spiritual gifts, including theirs.

Therefore, knowing our spiritual gifts is both a responsibility and an incredible privilege.

ENGAGE WITH A LOCAL CHURCH

Every believer has the responsibility to engage with a local congregation. You might think that everything I've written so far already communicates this message, but most of the time you'll find that this message needs its own specific teaching.

Of course, the very existence of spiritual gifts argues for a community outlet for those gifts. Paul says that the gifts are for the strengthening of the church (1 Cor. 14:26). He says they exist, "so that the body of Christ may be built up" (Eph. 4:12, NIV). Spiritual gifts don't exist in isolation from the community. They are not for our personal edification and comfort. God gives them to us not for our sake but for the sake of His people. Paul's whole picture of the church as a body of mutually inseparable parts in 1 Corinthians 12:12-14 leaves us with no other conclusion but that the church needs every member and every member needs the community of the church.

The author of Hebrews writes that Christian should not be, "giving up meeting together, as some are in the habit of doing, but encouraging one another—and all the more as you see the Day approaching" (Heb. 10:25, NIV). Gathering together is the chief means of encouraging others and of being encouraged. Every believer, including and maybe even especially the disabled, need this regular encouragement in the Lord. Nothing can replace the kind of encouragement we get from significant, regular and personal connection with other believers.

Peter uses a really interesting image to argue for sticking close to community. He says that we are, "like living stones... being built into a spiritual house" (1 Pet. 2:5, NIV). This image leaves us with the impression that each "living stone" is necessary for the whole building. How could it remain a standing, functional building if some of the stones were missing? And what purpose would the individual stones serve if they were not a part of the building? Peter goes on to call us a "priesthood" (vs. 5 and 9) and a "chosen people... a holy nation, God's special possession" (vs. 9, NIV). These are community words. They each conjure up the idea of a collective identity. Peter is saying that our identity as Christians is bound up with being part of a community of believers.

And of course, we wouldn't be able to obey Jesus' command to "love one another" (John 13:34, NIV) if we remained isolated from community. In fact, if we didn't engage with a local community, we'd be found guilty of resisting His prayer, "that all of them may be one, Father, just as you are in me and I am in you" (John 17:21).

It is undeniable that God gives every Christian the responsibility to engage in a local congregation. It is never easy for anyone, but I've already spent the first five chapters detailing how this is especially difficult for the disabled. And if someone is disabled, it is almost a guarantee that he has a story or two of just how difficult it has been to be involved in a local church. So when you're teaching this responsibility, you need to do it the right way.

Part of doing it the right way is of course to emphasize that it really is biblical and not optional. But you also need to communicate three related key ideas: it is beneficial, there is a lot of freedom for how to engage, and we need extra coaching for how to be self-advocates.

Local church engagement is undeniably beneficial, and you need to make the benefits a big part of how you teach this idea. But you also need to customize your teaching so that it fits the needs of the disabled. A family of non-disabled people might be attracted to a local church for completely different reasons than a disabled individual or a family with a disabled member. But there is still something about the community life that is attractive to both groups. Part of your job is to figure out what it is for the disabled.

For instance, will your church community help a new member grow in her relationship with Christ and in her progress toward Christ-likeness? More to the point, will your church help her grow in a way that is accessible? Are Braille materials readily available? Is all of the building accessible by wheelchair, or is the whole classroom wing off limits? It'll be hard for her to attend Sunday school or any other classes if she can't get to the classrooms. Is it OK if she comes late to the regular service, or is tardiness one of those unspoken rules that are unacceptable for your congregants to break? Will others view her as having the dignity of God's creation and the dignity of His beloved child, or will her second-class status be the real way most people silently regard her?

Questions like these are critical when you're trying to communicate that community life is beneficial. It might be easy for you to prove that community life is beneficial to a non-disabled person. But is it really beneficial in practical, felt ways for a disabled person? Do the benefits really outweigh the costs for the disabled at your church? It sounds a little crass to put it that way, but this really is part of the calculus a disabled person must think through before engaging in a local congregation. The fact is, community life does have a cost for the disabled. Jesus obviously thinks the benefits outweigh the costs, but does your congregation do a decent job of making that a reality for everyone?

And while you're talking about benefits, don't forget to emphasize how participation in a local congregation is a privilege as well as a responsibility. Many countries around the world actively prevent local church engagement by law. Thus, it is a remarkable privilege to live in a country that allows free association. All of us, disabled and non-disabled, need to be reminded of this fact.

The other key point you need to emphasize when teaching about this is that at your church, participation has a broad definition. There is a lot of freedom for engagement, and it can look a lot of different ways for different people. As I've stated earlier, disabled people often are on different schedules and often have lower levels of energy. We have various limitations that prevent us from doing certain things, or at least from doing them as often or as quickly as you do them. Some disabled people don't want to engage with a local church because they believe they'll be judged for not being able to do some things as quickly or as often as others. They think, "Why even try at that church? There, you need to be almost superhuman to be accepted and to be involved."

So, is there freedom at your church for involvement to look a lot of different ways for different people? Are there multiple levels of engagement? I ask because a lot of churches say there is freedom, but many times they have hidden and unspoken expectations that are a part of their culture. These expectations weed out those who can't keep up. For many disabled people, the expectations of the culture are just another barrier, though an invisible one.

For instance, a lot of churches expect certain tasks to get done at a very quick pace. Or they expect strict, weekly attendance. Or they have a culture that silently shames someone who shows up late. Or you're quietly looked down upon and not asked to be involved again if you miss one session of something. Or, when you can't keep up, you're secretly put the list that exists in every leader's head called the "eye-role list of exasperating, undependable people." Does any of this happen at your church? Or would I still be welcomed to be involved if I could only do it at my own pace and with an energy level that is manageable for me?

The third critical point is that you'll need to give the disabled some extra coaching for how to be self-advocates. Self-advocacy is something that most people learn to do on the playground as young children: "Hey, give that back! That's mine!" It is a necessary life skill for anybody. The disabled have usually learned how to be good self-advocates out in the world. We have to be or we won't survive. But church is often an entirely new and more confusing landscape for a lot of us and many disabled people need to refine their self-advocacy skills in order to engage in a local church.

Why is the church so different from the world when it comes to self-advocacy? Well, a lot of churches have a culture that is hypersensitive to rules of etiquette and politeness. This means that if I raise my voice a little too much at church others will frown on me. Or, if I ask a pointed, direct question, others who are used to indirect communication will feel uncomfortable. Or, if I have to take care of some physical function, others might think it is undignified of me. Many Christians associate these niceties of etiquette with following Jesus, and so they get very anxious if a disabled person sounds or looks out of the ordinary.

All this can make self-advocacy feel like a minefield for us. If too loud of a statement or too pointed of a request can earn disapproval instead of help, then why try? One of the main reasons that disabled people feel so alienated from churches is simply this sense that their efforts at self-advocacy lead to frustration and rejection instead of to open doors.

So your job is to help disabled people navigate this new culture of politeness and decorum. How do we get our needs met without offending people? How do we operate in this new landscape without stepping on a hidden mine?

Of course, it'll help if you can use your position of leadership to address this hypersensitive culture of your church. You can help your non-disabled churchgoers call into question why they so closely associate certain etiquette rules with following Jesus. You can point out how alienating that can be for some of us.

Teaching and doing all of this will help smooth the way for the disabled to engage with your local congregation.

ADVENTURE OUTSIDE OF YOUR COMFORT ZONE

One really important responsibility and privilege that you'll need to teach is to adventure outside of your comfort zone. In other words, you need to encourage disabled people to take risks and to push themselves to try new and different experiences. It is a responsibility because followers of Jesus are expected to be those who can bravely face what the world cannot. It is a privilege because God gives us this bravery and freedom as a free gift.

There are many reasons why everyone should take risks. It expands your horizons as a person. It forces you to grow. It increases your overall confidence. But this is especially important for disabled people to do. Sometimes, the natural limitations we face on a daily basis can get some of us to imagine that we've got more limitations than we really do. We can start to feel afraid of the dangers that surround us—dangers that can be worse and more numerous than the dangers that non-disabled people face. This can make us react to life by shrinking back and hiding. But fear tends to grow instead of decrease when we give in to it, so the only way to counteract it is to act in the opposite way. Thus, it becomes critical, especially for those of us who might be partially homebound or who have limited physical movement, to adventure outside of our comfort zone.

As with reconciliation, the Sawubona experiment showed that disabled people need a lot of coaching to take these new risks. During Sawubona, we coached each other on risk-taking. We would share our fears with one another and together as a group we would troubleshoot how to face those fears. This increased everyone's practical wisdom for how to do certain things. But best of all it increased everybody's confidence. We would cheer each other on before, during and after someone tried something new.

This benefit of Sawubona is another reason I so strongly recommended back in Chapter Five that you help disabled people network with each other. Other disabled people will have a greater ability to coach one another in risk-taking than you do. But you can duplicate some of these benefits when you teach this responsibility and privilege. As you teach about it, encourage disabled people to voice their fears and their sense of limitation. Talk openly about these perceived limits. It is important at this point not to criticize the fears or perceptions directly. Remember, it is tricky work to tease out the difference between real and perceived barriers, and you probably aren't in a position to do this work, especially if you are not disabled. You want to avoid invalidating the experiences of the disabled or you'll risk alienating them.

But you can encourage disabled people to take steps that counteract their fears. Coach them to ask themselves things like, "is there one thing I can do differently to face this fear?" Or "What is one step I can take today that will bring me closer to doing what I want to do?" You can do this gently and respectfully without calling into question their experiences or perceptions. For instance, you can say, "that must have been horrible when you were treated that way. What is one little step you can take to not remain a victim of that situation? How could you counteract that victimization by standing up for yourself next time?" Do you see? Combine validation with gentle urging in the direction of risk-taking.

Above all, keep reminding your disabled parishioners, "We do not belong to those who shrink back and are destroyed, but to those who have faith and are saved" (Heb. 10:39, NIV). It is a responsibility before God to take risks. Also remind them, "I can do all things through him who gives me strength" (Phil. 4:13, NIV). Risk-taking is one of the privileges of first-class citizens of heaven.

PUT THE BEST CONSTRUCTION ON EVERY INTERACTION

One final responsibility and privilege that every church needs to teach its disabled members is to put the best construction on every interaction. This basically means assuming that other people have the best intention, even when an interaction doesn't seem to go so well.

Let me be plain. Most of us with disabilities have had so many negative interactions because of our disabilities that we've become rather jaded about other peoples' intentions. We've all got stories of discrimination. We've all got stories of being belittled and thought of as incapable. We've all got stories of being patronized and being treated with paternalism. And these interactions never seem to follow a pattern. We'll have a positive interaction one moment with one person, and the next moment, seemingly out of nowhere, we'll have a negative interaction with a different person. This unpredictable pattern makes it so that we can't even protect ourselves from the next incident of discrimination because we can't know when it will happen next.

This has made most of us wonder if all non-disabled people have the same insensitivities or fearful attitudes toward the disabled. It can make us cynical about human nature, and it makes us feel self-protective and defensive. Some of us end up going around with a permanent cringe as we anticipate the bad things that will happen to us. It is like we're just waiting for the inevitable moment of discrimination or fear or insensitivity. No wonder so many disabled people are reluctant to join a local church.

But for Christian relationships to work, there needs to be trust. We need to relearn how to put the best construction possible on all our interactions in the church, even when they feel negative on the surface of things. We need to train ourselves to resist taking negative reactions personally.

Again, as with several of the other points I've made, this retraining is best done in a supportive network of other disabled people. Many of our Sawubona discussions were about how to handle perceived insults, slights and discrimination. One of us would come to the group and say, "hey guys, you'll never guess what happened to me today." We'd talk about the event and help each other sort through whether the slight was real or perceived, and how to react to it. A network like Sawubona is an essential part of training ourselves to put the best construction possible on all our interactions.

But just like with the last point, you can do some of this in your role as a church leader. You can teach disabled people the need for every Christian to assume the best about the intentions of others. You can impress upon them that even disabled people, who have encountered more than their fair share of discrimination and insults, have this responsibility.

You can help your disabled congregants see this as a privilege by helping them envision how much better a community could be if everyone were to give each other the benefit of the doubt. Help them to imagine what a privilege it is to be a part of a community in which everyone is regarded as so precious that we can think the best of each other even when we make mistakes. Because Christ "has destroyed the barrier, the dividing wall of hostility" (Eph. 2:14, NIV), Christians have the privilege of living in a community where trust dominates insensitivity and ignorance. We have the privilege of living in a community where mutual regard trumps exclusivity and discrimination.

CONCLUSION

I admit that the things in this chapter form a tall order. I'm recommending that you tweak and customize your teaching for your disabled congregants so that they can learn their responsibilities and privileges as first-class citizens of heaven. Is it extra work for you? Yes. But is the extra work worth it? Definitely. It empowers the disempowered and enables the disabled when you teach disabled Christians the duties and benefits of knowing and applying their new identity in Christ, of prayer, of forgiveness, of reconciliation, of identifying and using their spiritual gifts, of engaging with a local congregation, of adventuring outside of one's comfort zone and of assuming the best of others.

Chapter Seven

A Little Help with the Americans With Disabilities Act

One of the things I promised you at the beginning of this book was a lot of practical help for ministering to and with the disabled. One of the most helpful things I can give you is a quick, easy summary of the American's With Disability's Act (ADA). A lot of organizations worry about the ADA. They're afraid that they'll have to make a lot of really big and expensive changes in order to comply with it. Maybe you are also afraid of this for your church? I hope this chapter takes away some of the fear for you.

First, can I let you in on a little secret? Churches are technically exempt from the ADA. Yes, it's true. Religious organizations, private homes and private clubs are legally exempt from complying with the ADA, at least on a federal level for US churches.[36] Now, at this point maybe you're breathing a huge sigh of relief and you're thinking to yourself, "Whew! That little bit of information just saved us hundreds of thousands of dollars in expensive upgrades that we can't afford."

But here's the thing my dear fellow ministers in Christ: complying with the ADA, as far as it is possible and reasonable for your church, is simply the right thing to do. Even if the federal government will never hold you accountable for it, you should do what you can to comply with it.

It is the right thing to do because Jesus wants anybody to be able to encounter Him in your church building, without any barriers. It is the right thing to do because, as I've been saying over and over, God cares deeply for all those people who want to come to your church in person but who can't for one reason or another. It is the right thing to do because, well, you'd have to re-read almost this entire book to remember why it is the right thing to do.

But besides being the right thing to do, it is also about the most effective way to communicate, "We love you" to people with disabilities. When disabled people come into a building that is new to them, one of the first things they want to know about is how accessible it is. When they discover points that are not accessible, you might as well slam a door in their faces and tell them: "We don't want you here." That is the message we send when our buildings and facilities and events aren't accessible.

I know a lot of pastors who worry about the first-time experience of visitors. Maybe you're one of them, because you know that a person's first impression can determine if he or she will come back and give your church a second chance. Maybe as a church leader you regularly wonder things like, were the greeters friendly? Did the visitors find everything they needed? Were they welcomed warmly? What was the feeling they got when they first walked through the doors?

So to make this first time experience positive, many pastors work hard so that the building is clean; they work hard to train a group of conscientious ushers; they ensure that the greeters are above all friendly and helpful and that the signage around the building is clearly marked.

But what about the first-time experience of someone with

disabilities? What are you communicating with them when they first come through your front doors? Do they get the message that you'd love to have them join your extended spiritual family? Do they get the message that this community will be a place for them to flourish? Is it physically safe as well as spiritually safe?

Few things will help first-time visitors with disabilities better than your reasonable compliance with the ADA.

THE AMERICANS WITH DISABILITIES ACT was passed in 1980 as a way to make sure that disabled people could have access in all public facilities. It was expanded in 2008 to clarify more exactly what is meant by the term "disabled." But recently in 2018, the ADA has been making news headlines because the Trump administration is proposing changes that are raising concern among disability advocates.

The current ADA prohibits discrimination against people with disabilities in four main areas: employment, public services, public accommodations and communications.[37] The law around each of these four areas is called a "title." A fifth title makes sure that people with disabilities can always assert their rights. It prohibits coercing, threatening or retaliating against people with disabilities. It also prohibits doing these things against those who help people with disabilities.

I want you to understand a little about each of these five titles because that'll help you better understand why they are the right thing for you and for your church to champion.

HELP WITH TITLE I: EMPLOYMENT DISCRIMINATION

The first title is probably the one you've heard the most about. It is the prohibition against employment discrimination. Most churches, even though they're not required to do to this, include in their employment policies a statement about not discriminating based on a physical disability. A lot of churches worry about this part because they think the government will force them to hire someone who would not be a fit for their particular church. I've heard pastors worry out loud about things like, "What if the government makes me hire someone from a different religion?!" But the US government has always been careful to let private organizations hire whomever they want to hire. I don't think you have much to worry about along these lines, especially if you lead a church.

The main thing this title asks of employers is to make what are called "reasonable accommodations" for employees and potential employees. The law gives some examples of reasonable accommodations. For instance: "restructuring jobs, making worksites and work stations accessible, modifying schedules, providing services such as interpreters, and modifying equipment and policies."[38]

What does this mean? Let's say you hire a church secretary who uses a wheel chair. First of all, can she physically get into the church building and into the church office? And once she's in, can she navigate around the office and wherever else she needs to go? Is the phone within easy reach? Are the file cabinets positioned so that she can access them while still staying in her chair? Can she get to and from the bathroom? Is the bathroom itself accessible once she's in there? This the most basic meaning of the term "accessible."

What about this language regarding "restructuring jobs" and "modifying schedules?" This means taking into account how her disability might affect the job performance itself. Maybe she gets more exhausted than someone without a disability and needs to take a longer mid-day break. Is it really a sacrifice for you to let her have a 45 minute lunch break instead of 30? Or maybe mornings are especially difficult for her, so you let her do the first few hours of work from home. Would it really reduce productivity if you let her do that? Maybe the previous secretary was required to cross the building to do the photocopying. Would it be possible to move the photocopier closer to the secretary's desk?

I've heard a lot of church leaders object at this point, saying, "Why should we make all these changes for an employee? Aren't they supposed to help us and make our jobs easier instead of the reverse?"

You're correct that employees are hired to make things better for the employer. Otherwise, you wouldn't hire them. But let me ask you a couple of questions. First, like you've heard me say so many times in this book, how do you know what this employee is capable of until you give her a chance? Maybe she'll prove to be a bigger blessing to you and to the church than you'd imagined possible? Maybe she'll be better at what she does than the previous church secretary? As I've chronicled in story after story already, when given a chance many people with disabilities will surprise you with the quality of their contributions.

Often, the contributions of disabled people far outweigh the minor adjustments you need to make in order to accommodate them. Yes, it is inconvenient for you to spend a couple of hours moving that photocopier. But who knows how efficient and effective the new secretary will prove to be? Maybe she'll surpass your expectations and you won't even remember the two hours you spent getting the copier moved in comparison with what she's accomplished. But you won't know any of that until you give someone the chance.

Second, if part of your job is to model the coming of the Kingdom of God, and if part of the church's job is to demonstrate how the presence of Jesus' Kingdom makes a practical difference in the world right now, then what are you really losing by making your workplace a little more accessible? What better models God's rule and reign on earth? What says, "God loves His people" better and more effectively than a workplace that makes room for anybody to work there. If the Gospel is essentially a story of accessibility (the accessibility of God's people to His love through Jesus' sacrifice), what better communicates this than an accessible work place?

This first title also talks about making hiring practices more accessible for people with disabilities. Now, obviously if you need a maintenance fellow who can climb a 40 foot latter to change light bulbs, go ahead and hire a person who can do that. But when you hire for something, do you even consider disabled applicants? Or do you dismiss them before even thinking of them as a possibility?

Even though your church will never get prosecuted for hiring discrimination, this isn't about avoiding negative legal consequences. This is about cultivating the right attitude in your heart as a representative of God. And the right attitude is to be open to whomever God might bring across your path for a particular job. Remember all the people like Gideon and Samson and David who didn't appear to be qualified for the job of leading Israel? Remember how surprised people were when God picked them? Be open to God's surprises. Be open to God sending you a Gideon or a Samson or a David.

HELP WITH TITLE II: PUBLIC SERVICES

The second title says that all public (federal, state and local) services, "cannot deny services to people with disabilities or deny participation in programs and activities that are available to people without disabilities."[39] This mainly impacts transportation. Thus, all the rules about accessibility on public buses, trains and so on come out of this title. Not surprisingly, the U.S. Department of Transportation, along with the U.S. Department of Justice, are the main enforcers of this title. The U.S. Department of Education also enforces some of these regulations, because this title also controls disability access in public education.[40]

How does this impact you? Again, you're not required legally to do anything with this part of the law. But does your church bus have a lift for people in wheel chairs? If that's an unreasonable cost, do you have another way to transport people with mobility restrictions? Some churches have budgets that are too small to justify adding a lift to the church bus (if they even have a church bus). But they do have a little army of volunteers who pick up wheelchair bound members on Sunday morning. Who in your church has a little extra room in their cars to spare, and who'd be blessed to participate more actively in ministry?

Besides just getting to church, are all your church activities accessible? I know about a small church that held an annual church picnic at a local park. But the park wasn't very accessible so that those people in wheelchairs were forced to miss out on this event. This was sad because the picnic was a huge highlight for everyone else in the church. This left many people feeling excluded and hurt. Eventually, the church switched locations and mended their ways.

Churches that make disabled people feel welcome think about accessibility in everything they do. Can everyone get to that Bible study who wants to? Can everyone listen to that sermon who wants to? Could a young person with a disability go on the youth mission trip if he desired? Churches that do disability ministry well are always asking themselves these kinds of questions.

HELP WITH TITLE III: PUBLIC ACCOMMODATIONS

The third title sounds similar to Title Two but has some important differences. It requires that whenever anyone builds a new building or structure, there have to be modifications that make that building accessible for people with disabilities (for any people, not just employees). Unlike Title Two, Title Three affects privately owned buildings and facilities. For existing facilities, "barriers to services must be removed if readily achievable." This "readily achievable" language means that there can be exceptions for historic preservation situations and for unique situations like non-standard architecture. But it also means that if at all possible, buildings should be made accessible.

Again, churches aren't required to comply with these regulations. But can I tell you something interesting? I have a friend who recently visited Ebenezer Baptist Church in Atlanta, Georgia. That is the church where Martin Luther King, Jr. grew up and got his start in ministry as an associate pastor, mentored by the senior pastor, his father Martin Luther King, Sr. until he got his own congregation in Montgomery, Alabama in 1954. If any building qualifies as an exemption to Title III because of a historic preservation designation, it is Ebenezer Baptist. Not only is it a beautiful older building (they began building it in 1877), but it has had an enormous impact on history, to say the least. There is a strong argument for keeping it just like it was when Martin Luther King, Jr. preached there in the early 1950s. With great support from almost any reasonable person, you could rationally recommend making no accessibility modifications to that building.

But guess what? Beginning in 2001 Ebenezer Baptist put in a wheelchair accessible elevator, greatly altering its original look and structure. Like many church buildings from that era, its main sanctuary was built a full story above street level. To get to it, you had to climb up a full flight of steps. But now anyone can access this sanctuary that has played such in important role in US (even world) history. What's more, they installed the new elevator in the front entrance. A lot of historic buildings, when they do get around to installing an elevator, put it far in the back so that it doesn't disrupt the original look of the building or inconvenience people coming through the main doors. But Ebenezer put it right in the front.

What do you think? Does the presence of an elevator damage the inspiring nature of Ebenezer Baptist? Does it reduce Martin Luther King Jr's legacy in some way? Or does it actually enhance that legacy?

What will better accessibility do to the legacy of your church?

HELP WITH TITLE IV: COMMUNICATIONS

Title IV is all about communications. Specifically, it says that telecommunications companies have to offer their services to people who need hearing impaired devices. If these companies offer services to the general public, then they must offer comparable services to those who need modifications for hearing impairment. These devices are called TTYs or TDDs. TTY stands for TeleTYpwriter. TDD stands for Telecommunication Device for the Deaf. TTY/TDD technology paved the way for texting technology that is now used everywhere by just about everyone.

You might think that Title IV has nothing to do with your church. But think for a moment about the importance of communication in your church. Think about what happens when people miss your Sunday morning sermon? What happens when they don't read your bulletin? What happens when they don't hear your announcements? What if they ignore your emails? When people don't have access to all these forms of communication, what becomes of their place in your church? What happens to the quality of their participation in your community? Would you even call such a person a full member in good standing if they are completely cut off from all your vital communications?

Do you see what I'm getting at? Communication plays a key role in your church community. You could almost say that it is at the center of everything. What happens to any church without communication? Communication helps everyone feels heard. It helps everyone understand what is going on. It guarantees that your message spreads and has an impact for now and for eternity.

You could even argue that the Gospel itself doesn't go anywhere or make a difference in anyone's life without good communication. After all, the Gospel is the heart of God's communication with us.

Now imagine that some in your community, or some who would be in your community if they could, are cut off from decent communication. Imagine their experience of community life in this situation. Imagine how they would or wouldn't encounter the Gospel in this situation.

The creators of the ADA knew that a lack of access to communication was one of the biggest causes of isolation for people with disabilities. Poor communication prevents many people from being a part of a community. This in turn makes communications a major cause of discrimination faced by the disabled. If certain people can't communicate, if they can't understand the communications of others and if they can't make their communication heard, they become vulnerable and they are cut off from many of the benefits of a community.

So here's my question for you. What does your church offer people who communicate differently from the mainstream?

Do you have sign language interpreters? Do you have TTY/ TDD devices of some sort? What do you do to bridge the communication barriers?

At this point you might say, "Now Theresa, this is unreasonable. We don't even have people with hearing impairment at our church. Why would we invest in these things?"

My question back to you would be, "why do you think they are not at your church?"

And it isn't just people who are hearing impaired that you need to think about. If a person reaches a certain level of blindness, he can't read your bulletins and other published materials. Will this parishioner have access to Braille at your church? If not Braille, what will you do to cross this communication divide? Doesn't the Gospel demand that we do whatever it takes to cross these divides?

HELP WITH TITLE V: PROTECTIONS

This last title is kind of a catchall to ensure that no one who is disabled faces discrimination. It prohibits coercing, threatening or retaliating against disabled people. It also prohibits coercing, threatening or retaliating against those who help people with disabilities. This fifth title was created in case people with disabilities (and their allies) face opposition when they attempt to assert their rights under the other four titles. It is a necessary part of the ADA because we really do encounter opposition to our rights.

The federal government won't prosecute you and your church for failing to protect the disabled. But what does God think and feel when we fail to protect the disabled among us?

When we don't stand up for them? When we allow a culture in our churches that coerces, threatens or retaliates against them?

What if your church became known as a place where those with disabilities find protection? Advocacy? Solidarity in the face of opposition? What if the disabled who lived nearby gradually began to learn that your church was a place where others would stick up for them and help fight their battles? What if it were known as a truly safe place for them?

Now you understand the ADA a little better. Maybe this chapter mainly made you feel relieved that federal law doesn't require your church to comply with it. But think about how this law carefully protects disabled people from all the subtle forms of discrimination. Think about how it makes a way for them to truly flourish. It does this because it thoroughly covers so many critical parts of life for disabled people. Each part of the law has been carefully laid out so this could happen.

Don't you want your church to be a place where anyone can flourish in God? Your church can be just such a place for people with disabilities if you would use the ADA as a guide for a full-fledged disability ministry. If you're serious about ministering to and with people with disabilities, then each of the five titles will help you understand the best way to go forward. The ADA will help you think through employment, services, accommodations, communications and the prevention of discrimination. Any good disability ministry includes all five of these areas.

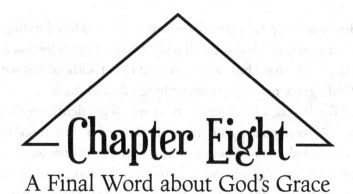

Chapter Eight

A Final Word about God's Grace

There is a song, "Table of Grace," by Randy Phillips, Shawn Craig and Dan Dean. It describes a place where we all can come and be treated as equals. There is plenty of food, love and most of all, grace. As we come to the end of this book I want to impress upon you the absolute importance of grace.

Throughout the Bible, God offers grace over and over. I'm thinking of famous passages like Romans 3:24 or 4:16, Ephesians 2:8-9 or Titus 2:11. I know you can think of dozens and dozens more. God knows we do not deserve it but He still offers it over and over.

I depend on this grace every day. I wouldn't be able to make it without the grace. I certainly wouldn't be able to minister like I do without it. In fact, I have this little daily practice in which I "add extra grace" into my day. You see, as I approach obstacles in ministry or in life, I mentally rehearse putting "on the full armor of God" (Ephesians 6:10-20, NIV). And when I do this I "add extra grace" for myself and for all of those around me. Yes, I begin with myself. I say to myself something like: "Stay firm in who you are and in what God has called you for. Making yourself vulnerable is typically part of the call and as you feel the sting of hurt or rejection, bless yourself with abundant grace for you and for those who have hurt you." I couldn't do it without this sense of God's grace permeating everything I do and think.

I'll tell you a little story about my dependence on God's grace. Several years ago Ken and I attended a conference that was intended to equip people to minister to the disabled. I was excited to get refueled and to network with more people who were passionate like us. Well, that weekend still brings tears to my eyes because, as you can guess, all did not go as advertised.

The conference started with a luncheon where we were treated like royalty and encouraged to make friends at our table. The lady next to me asked what my disabilities were. I let her know that I was very hard of hearing and blind. But as the room got louder and louder, I struggled to continue a conversation with her. I had asked the conference leadership ahead of time for accommodations like a personal listening device. This kind of device typically involves a little microphone that would work with my hearing aids. It is something I can quickly pass to another person with whom I am engaged in conversation. It makes interactions flow a lot more smoothly.

But they said they forgot my accommodations. So I went to my back up plan of action: I asked my hubby to translate with sign. Sometimes we find ourselves in these sorts of situations in which he has to take on a caregiver role. He does this effortlessly and I am blessed when he does it. It not only affirms me, but it provides me some dignity in awkward situations.

But guess what? This woman became annoyed with me. She got annoyed because, as she said, "one minute you can hear and the next you can't." Then she actually told me to try harder and perhaps I would realize the disabilities were in my head! I was so hurt. It left me feeling pretty overwhelmed. I simply started praying and asking for God's grace. Wow, did I need it right at that moment.

I do realize that the presentation of my disabilities can be a little bewildering. It actually happens quite a bit that people get confused by me. You see, when I first meet somebody, I seem like an extravert with lots of humor and enthusiasm. But if you really get to know me you'd realize I am painfully shy. You'd discover that I tend to present myself like an extrovert so that people will want to continue talking with me. Generally I recognize that other peoples' investment into a conversation may be much higher then mine. They may have to repeat things for me. They may have to speak into a microphone. They may have to wait till I find someone to interpret for us. I realize that this is hard work for them, so I go out of my way to make them feel as comfortable as I can. I try to put the habits I have to control, like shyness, out of the way. I see it as a way to help equalize this investment and thus the playing field.

I know this can be confusing. I think that was why this lady didn't understand when she interacted with me at the lunch table. She had first encountered me as someone who didn't seem to need any accommodations. But then she encountered me as someone who did. It didn't make sense to her, just like it doesn't always make sense to a lot of people. I get it.

But I was still so hurt! I felt like she was calling me a delusional liar. But God provided the grace I needed a few moments later. During the next break, another conference attendee approached me. She said that she had noticed me looking sad and she asked if there was some way she could pray for me. This opened the floodgates and my tears started running freely. This is not in my character at all to just cry in front of total strangers. I had grown up with the rugged, independent attitude of Vermont in which you keep hurts to yourself and present a stoic front.

This woman was a grace from God, and I still treasure her today. We keep in contact to this day and we pray for one another. Her simple but powerful gesture of asking how to pray for me was huge! Her act reminded me that God knew I was hurting. That's how I experienced God's grace in that moment. It is just one example of how I rely on His grace every day.

But God had even greater grace for me in that day. While this woman was praying for me, God reminded me that these other attendees were hurting as well as I was. He reminded me that even people like the woman who initially hurt my feelings at the lunch table might be hurting from something too. It may have been her hurt that caused her to be so insensitive toward me.

I realized in that moment that even though we were all at this conference to prepare to minister to vulnerable people, for whatever reason the attendees felt vulnerable too. This population of disabled people, who were supposed to be the beneficiaries of this conference, made these leaders and ministers themselves feel scared and anxious. It was this sense of vulnerability that had made the lady at the lunch table be controlling instead of compassionate. She tried to solve my problems with unsolicited words of shaming. She hoped to "fix" me by giving me a pep talk. That's a behavior that comes from anxiety and from a feeling of vulnerability.

But God's grace gave me perspective and even compassion for those who had hurt me. What a wonderful God we serve!

How could that first lady at the lunch table have helped me instead of hurt me? She would have helped if she had just honestly admitted her confusion. That would have allowed me to explain things to her. She could have simply said something like, "I am so confused Theresa. I don't understand why at first you could hear me and now you can't. It doesn't make sense to me." Then I would have had an opening to clear up the confusion.

Instead, probably out of her own sense of vulnerability, she tried to correct me.

This part of my story re-emphasizes that you do not have to understand any parts of a disability to help. You don't need to understand the accommodations for a particular disability. All you have to do is be ready to respond with grace. With the help of God's grace, remember that the person with whom you are talking is a precious gift from God. Maybe that person presents her or his disability in a way that is unclear to you, like I did with that lady at the lunch table. Instead of trying to alleviate your confusion by controlling the other person, just ask for clarification. Don't shrug them off as if they are faking it.

The conference continued. Little did I know that I would need to depend heavily on God's grace even more that weekend. There was a comedian providing evening entertainment. Apparently many of the people attending were either caregivers to the disabled or they were able-bodied persons. I could tell because many of the jokes the comedian kept telling were about a disabled person's mishaps. They highlighted how the caregiver fixed it all and became the hero. The jokes seemed targeted to pleasing caregivers and not care-recipients. I'll admit that many of the items that the comedian mentioned were completely accurate. But the portrayal of caregiver heroism was hurtful to me that night. I knew even in that moment that the hurt was unintentional. But hurt is hurt. Yep, you guessed it—more tears.

Ken and I went for a walk to pray about it. We asked God to give me understanding about why I felt so persecuted. Then, all of sudden, one of the backstage helpers approached me and asked if he could pray with me. It was an incredible uplift from God right when I needed it most! He started praying with no explanations from me about what was wrong with me. It showed me that God is truly in control. More grace from God!

This kind of grace—an unexpected expression of care and concern—is our biggest weapon against the feeling of persecution that so many disabled people feel. After reading this book, I challenge you to be that back stage guy. Be that guy even though you are a pastor or a lay leader in your church and your job might give you a million other things to do today. If you see someone in your church hurting, offer to pray right then and there. Offer to pray no matter what, even without knowing why the person is hurting. The power of doing this is that you have just invited God into the interaction. You've opened the door to God's grace. That means the other person will experience God's gracious touch no matter what has happened to him. Somehow, God is going to come through for that person with His grace in one way or another. Of course I recommend using the normal cautions if the person is the opposite gender. But that can be overcome easily by grabbing someone else in the church to join in the prayer.

Praying like this will always be the best way to welcome anyone to God's table of grace. We are so dependent on God's grace. We are so dependent in fact that I believe the very best thing we can do for anybody is to give that person a foretaste of God's grace.

How do we give people foretastes of God's grace? Let me answer by reminding you of the metaphor of the Great Banquet. Earlier I mentioned the song "Table of Grace" by Phillips, Craig and Dean. The table of grace in the song speaks of the Great Banquet. Of all the wonderful metaphors God has given us, I think this one best describes the goal of this book.

First, remember that all the followers of Jesus are headed to this Great Banquet. This is true if we're able-bodied or disabled. It is the destination of the great "race" (Hebrews 12:1-3) in which all of us are moving closer to Jesus. The Great Banquet, in which we dine with Jesus Himself, is the prize of that race. While we run this race we are constantly surrounded by Biblical giants like Moses, Elijah and David (Hebrews 11). They are all witnessing this race. We are also running with our fellow believers. In the same way that we can learn so much from the Biblical giants cheering us on, we can also learn from and rely on our fellow runners. After we make the decision to run for Jesus, we become part of a team that loves, encourages and strengthens each other in the race toward the Banquet.

Some of us in this race may be homeless, so others of us provide shelter. Some may be parentless and so others of us provide a family. Some may be unable to see the goal, either because of a physical affliction or because of a spiritual one. So others of us help them keep their eyes focused on Jesus. Some may need to be carried, so we carry them. Others may be afraid and run the wrong way. So we need to gently steer them in the right direction. Some people may be carried, others use a wheelchair, and still others require communication devices. No matter how some people are "running," we are there to help one another run the race to the Banquet. And we're there to bring new people into the race so that we can all end up at the throne of Jesus.

Part of how we help people run the race, and part of how we bring in new people to the race, is to give them a taste of the Great Banquet. We do that in a lot of ways, but one of the easiest ways is simple hospitality and fellowship. When we graciously invite others to sit with us to eat, we give them a sneak peek, a foretaste, of the Great Banquet itself.

This simple hospitality starts right where you are. Right now as I write this I am picturing a table with some coffee and snacks and comfy chairs like we find all over the country today in our local churches. Are you picturing it with me? Gathered there are old and young, wealthy and poor. They have a common goal of enjoying a snack with fellow believers. I have sat at many such tables and interacted with many different kinds of people. There is no perfect three-step process for helping a new person feel welcome, but everyone feels God's grace when we sincerely show that we are happy for more company. Imagine a company of people who are glad that you've joined them. Feel the warmth of their embrace and friendship.

Now picture yourself at such a snack table in another church and this time picture yourself with a disability. What are you feeling? How are others treating you? Is anyone making eye contact? Is someone giving you a little too much attention? Is someone else treating you like you are five and not fifty? All of these people may be well-intentioned in their efforts to show you hospitality, but they also need you to be gracious with them since they may not know how to interact with you. You're not just a new person—you're a new person with a disability to boot. You understand that all these factors can make it awkward for them.

But it is awkward for you too. The interaction and the people are new to you also. You realize it is quite possible that you could snap at someone in a socially unacceptable manner or make an unkind comment if things get too overwhelming as they sometimes do. After all, it has happened before and it will likely happen again. How will you excuse yourself if you need to so that you can recover from an awkward interaction? It is not as easy for you to do this as it is for them.

I bring this up because as an able-bodied leader, you need to decide how you will make a disabled person feel comfortable in a new situation like this. Even though it is awkward for you, it is even more awkward for them. How will you give them a foretaste of the Great Banquet with your warm hospitality?

This is a really important exercise for you to do in your imagination. It will awaken empathy in your heart for the disabled. I teach a master's level class at the seminary on disability awareness. For one of my projects I ask my students to find a family affected by a disability and interview them. It has to be a family they do not know. This creates so much tension and anxiety for most of my students. To help students who feel especially taken aback by this assignment, I challenge them to take a drive and visit an unfamiliar church and sit down for snacks. I challenge them to put on new lenses and notice if anyone around them may be affected by a disability. So far, all my students have come back with life-changing experiences. Yes, there are disabilities in every church, including yours.

If you're going to put on new lenses, imagine yourself at that fellowship table. Have you made it a "table of grace"? Is it a foretaste of God's Great Banquet? Would disabled newcomers catch a glimpse of that Banquet when they sit with you?

Now let's move from a snack table in the back of our church to a related symbol of our faith, the communion table. Let's remember that we are celebrating the incredible love Jesus has for us. We know that we are saved through the shedding of His blood. His act of complete surrender came with the cost of His own brokenness. As we take communion and we pray with the elements, we should take comfort and strength from the fact that God sent His son and allowed Him to be broken for us. The next time we receive the broken bread let's recall that a broken Jesus has the power to heal all of our transgressions here on earth. He did this in order to reach us and save each of us who believe. Let's not deny that God intends this power for the broken members of our church family. And let us not deny that this power and God's glory can come through these broken members of the family.

Let us take communion by witnessing to the power and love of our broken Savior. Let us see this power and love that is available for and through all people, regardless of their abilities and disabilities.

About the Author

Rev. Dr. Theresa C. Taylor has a passion for disability advocacy. She and her husband founded Seek the Son Ministries Inc. which focuses on bringing the saving power of Jesus to the disabled. Theresa is deaf-blind and understands the obstacles that may hinder participation in a local church. Theresa also has a Doctorate of Ministry in Pastoral care along with being an ordained  pastor through International Ministerial Fellowship. This background allows her to provide a great support to church leadership to overcome the obstacles to welcoming the disabled to our local churches. Theresa has an extraordinary gift for teaching in a way that encourages readers to "want to learn". Theresa acknowledges that change is often tough in church communities. She challenges each of us to fulfill God's desire to welcome all to the great banquet including those with disabilities.

A Little List of More Resources

I thought it would be helpful to include this short list of some of the resources on disability ministry that I've used over the years. There are so many wonderful books and articles out there already. I didn't want to keep them to myself. These are in addition to the wonderful resources I've included in the End Notes (starting on the next page). You'll find some of these to be kind of academic, but many of them are accessible to anybody. Some of these resources are Christian. Some are secular. Enjoy!

Seek the Son Ministries: Reaching the Disabled with the Saving Power of Jesus Christ, http://www.seektheson.org/

Brown, Elizabeth. *The Disabled Disciple: Ministering in a Church Without Barriers*. Ligouri: Liguori Publications, 1997.

Chivers, Charlie. *Compel Them To Come In: Reaching People with Disabilities through the Local Church*. Bloomington: AuthorHouse, 2010.

Creamer, Deborah, *The Withered Hand of God: Disability and Theological Reflections*. PhD diss., Iliff School of Theology and University of Denver Joint PhD program, 2004.

Davis, Lennard J. *Enforcing Normalcy: Deafness and the Body*. New York: Verso, 1995.

Demmons, Tracy. "The Meaning and Message of Embodiment and Disability." MA. thesis, Acadia University, 2004.

Disabled World: Towards Tomorrow. "Definitions of the Models of Disability." http://www.disabled-world.com/definitions/disability-models.php.

Eiseland, Nancy. "What is Disability" *Stimulus* 6 (November, 1998): 24-30.

Haslan, Molly Claire. "Dethroning Rationality: A Theological Anthropology of/for Individuals with Intellectual Disabilities." PhD diss., Vanderbilt University, 2007.

Pearson, James. *Exceptional Teaching: A Comprehensive Guide for Including Students with Disabilities*. Cincinnati: Standard Publishing Company, 2002.

Reynolds, Thomas E. *Vulnerable Communities: A Theology of Disability and Hospitality*. Grand Rapids: Brazos Press, 2008.

Shapiro Joseph. *No Pity: People with Disabilities Forging a New Civil Rights Movement*. New York: Three Rivers Press, 1994.

Vanier, Jean. *From Brokenness to Community*. Mahwah: Paulist Press, 1992.

_____. *Encountering the Other*. Mahwah: Paulist Press, 2006.

Notes

CHAPTER ONE:

1   "World Facts and Statistics on Disabilities and Disability Issues," *Disabled World: Toward Tomorrow*, accessed September 1, 2011, http://www.disabled-world.com/disability/statistics/.

2   Ibid.

3   Ibid.

4   Ibid.

5   Ibid.

6   Joni Earekson Tada and Jack S. Oppenhuizen, "Hidden and Forgotten People: Ministry Among People with Disability," Lausanne Occasional Paper #35B, *Lausanne Committee for World Evangelization* (2004). http://www. lausanne.org/docs/2004forum/LOP35B_IG6B.pdf (accessed March, 2013)..

7   Ibid.

8   Ibid.

9   Ibid.

10   Unless otherwise noted, all references to Holy Scripture are taken from THE HOLY BIBLE, NEW INTERNATIONAL VERSION®, NIV® Copyright© 1973, 1978, 1984, 2011 by Biblica, Inc.® Used by permission. All rights reserved worldwide.

CHAPTER TWO:

11   Daniel Goleman, "What Predicts Your Success? It's Not Your IQ." July 17, 2014, accessed August 26, 2015, http://www.danielgoleman.info/daniel-goleman-what-predicts-success-its-not-your-iq/

12 Nancy Eiseland, *A Disabled God: Toward a Liberating Theology of Disability* (Nashville: Abington Press, 1994), 23.

13 A. T. Robertson, *Word Pictures in the New Testament*, (Nashville: Broadman Press, 1933), e-book, LOGOS Bible Library, accessed May 28, 2012.

14 David E. Garland, *Vol. 29, 2 Corinthians. The New American Commentary* (Nashville: Broadman and Holman Publishers, 1999), e-book, LOGOS Bible Library, accessed May 28, 2012.

15 Eiseland, 28.

CHAPTER THREE:

16 All names of individuals have been changed to protect confidentiality.

17 James W. Albers and Robert Smith, preparers, "Writings in the Field of American Lutheranism, 1989," *Lutheran Historical Conference*, http://www.luthhist.org/bibliography/1989.html, (accessed May, 2011).

18 The Evangelical Church of America, "Social Issues", http://www.elca.org/What-We-Believe/Social-Issues/Messages/Human-Disabilities/A-Brief-History.aspx#_edn9 (accessed November 26, 2012).

19 Ibid.

20 Deborah Creamer, *Disability and Christian Theology: Embodied Limits and Constructive Possibilities*, in the American Academy of Religion Series (New York: Oxford University Press, 2009), 15.

21 Joseph Shapiro, *No Pity: People with Disabilities Forging a New Civil Rights Movement* (New York: Three Rivers Press, 1994), 43.

22 Shapiro, 13.

23 Creamer, *Disability and Christian Theology*, 16.

24 Bryan Kemp, "Depression as a Secondary Condition in People with Disabilities," Appendix N in *Workshop on Disability in America: A New Look*, Marilyn J. Field, Alan M. Jette, and Linda Martin, eds. (Washington, D.C.: National Academies Press, 2006) 234.

25 Stanley Hauerwas, *Critical Reflections Of Stanley Hauerwas' Theology Of Disability: Disabling Society, Enabling Theology*, (Binghampton, NY: Hawthorn Pastoral Press, 2004), 51.

CHAPTER FOUR:

26 Some of the books I used were *Religion Online: Finding Faith on the Internet*, by Lorne Dawson and Doug Cowan; *Virtual Community: The*

Homesteading on the Electronic Frontier by Howard Rheingold; *My Space to Sacred Space: God for a New Generation,* by Christian Piatt.

27 Orland Bishop, "Sawubona," *Global Oneness Project,* http://www. globalonenessproject.org/library/interviews/sawubona (accessed November 2012).

28 http://www.rita.dot.gov/bts/sites/rita.dot.gov.bts/files/publications/ freedom_to_travel/html/data_analysis.html

29 There are several interesting books on this topic. One that helped me launch into this topic was by Jonathon Wilson-Hartgrove, entitled *New Monasticism: What It Has to Say to Today's Church* (Ada, MI: Brazos Press, 2008).

CHAPTER FIVE:

30 Warren W. Wiersbe, *Wiersbe's Expository Outlines on the Old Testament* (Wheaton: Victor Books, 1993), e-book, LOGOS Bible Library, (accessed May 6, 2012).

31 Howard Ross, *Reinventing Diversity: Transforming Organizational Community to Strengthen People, Purpose, and Performance* (Lanham, MD: Rowman and Littlefield Publishers, 2011), xi.

32 Ibid., 119.

33 Taylor Cox Jr., *Cultural Diversity in Organizations: Theory, Research, & Practice* (San Francisco, CA: Berrett-Koehler, 1994), 11.

34 Ibid., 36.

35 Ibid., 33-34.

CHAPTER SEVEN:

36 The United States Access Board, Chapter 1, "Using the ADA Standards," https://www.access-board.gov/guidelines-and-standards/buildings- and-sites/about -the-ada-standards/guide-to-the-ada-standards/ chapter-1-using-the-ada-standards

37 "The Americans with Disabilities Act: A Brief Overview," US Department of Labor, https://askjan.org/links/adasummary.htm

38 Ibid.

39 Ibid.

40 US Department of Labor, https://www.dol.gov/general/topic/ disability/ada

Printed in the United States
By Bookmasters